One-Stitch BABY KNITS

Published 2019—IMM Lifestyle Books
www.IMMLifestyleBooks.com

IMM Lifestyle Books are distributed in the UK by
Grantham Book Service, Trent Road, Grantham,
Lincolnshire, NG31 7XQ.

In North America, IMM Lifestyle Books are
distributed by Fox Chapel Publishing, 903 Square
Street, Mount Joy, PA 17552,
www.FoxChapelPublishing.com.

ISBN 978-1-5048-0110-2

Library of Congress Cataloging-in-Publication Data

Names: Pierce, Val, author.
Title: One-stitch baby knits / Val Pierce.
Description: Mount Joy : IMM Lifestyle Books,
   2019. | Includes index.
Identifiers: LCCN 2019006106 (print) | LCCN
   2019010676 (ebook) | ISBN 9781607656623
   (ebook) | ISBN 9781504801102
Subjects: LCSH: Knitting--Patterns. | Infants'
   clothing.
Classification: LCC TT825 (ebook) | LCC TT825
   .P4918 2019 (print) | DDC 746.43/2--dc23
LC record available at https://lccn.loc.gov/
   2019006106

We are always looking for talented authors. To
submit an idea, please send a brief inquiry to
acquisitions@foxchapelpublishing.com.

Printed in Singapore
10 9 8 7 6 5 4 3 2 1

This book has been published with the intent to
provide accurate and authoritative information in
regard to the subject matter within. While every
precaution has been taken in the preparation of
this book, the author and publisher expressly
disclaim any responsibility for any errors,
omissions, or adverse effects arising from the use
or application of the information contained herein.

One-Stitch
BABY KNITS

22 EASY PATTERNS
for Adorable Garments and Accessories Using Garter Stitch

Val Pierce

IMM **lifestyle**
books ™

Read. Learn. Do What You Love.

Beginner

30 Geometric Blanket

34 Easy Burp Cloth

38 Tickled Pink Bootie and
Headband Set

42 Bunny Earflap Hat

Intermediate

54 Color-Block Hooded Scarf

58 Navy and Speckle
Striped Booties

62 Pink Ombré Baby Bib

66 Sleepy Babies Blanke

82 Christmas Shoes

86 Ducky Snuggle Blankie

90 Toasty Mittens
on a Rope

Experienced

104 Striped Yoke Cardigan

110 Newborn Diaper Cover, Hat,
and Booties

116 Teddy Bear Romper

6 T-Shaped Sweater and Simple Shoes

51 Simple Pom-Pom Hat

72 Pinafore Dress

78 Sailboat Bib

94 Navy Striped Bib

98 Sleepy Cow Hat and Drawstring Mittens

122 Under-the-Sea Hooded Jacket

130 Little Rosebud Wrap Set

Contents

Introduction

Knitting is a fun and relaxing craft that has increased in popularity over the years. Once deemed a craft for older folks, it has now become a big favorite with the younger community. Even schools are introducing the craft into their curriculum.

The yarns available to knitters in stores and online are many and varied, and the array of sumptuous colors and textures to choose from makes creating your own knitted projects a sheer delight.

Once you have mastered the very basics of casting on and off, the knit stitch, and making a simple square, you will be keen to start knitting your very own projects. With this in mind, I have designed 22 easy projects to knit for babies. Using different yarn changes, yarn textures, and the odd slipstitch, you will be able to create blankets, hats, sweaters, and mittens that will look anything but simple.

The majority of projects in this book have little or no shaping. They have no neckbands to pick up and no front bands to sew on, which means they can be attempted by even the novice knitter. That said, it must be stated that there are also some designs included in this book that are better attempted by more experienced knitters. A star rating will show you which projects you should attempt first. As you progress with your knitting skills, you can move on to the more complex designs. Whatever your knitting skills are now, I feel sure that you will find something among the designs that you will love!

Hints, Tips, and Techniques

Here are some helpful hints, tips, and techniques to get you started—including a quick rundown of basic materials, accessories, and techniques such as stitches, casting on, binding off, and completing your project.

Materials and Accessories

YARNS

It can be quite daunting for a new knitter to decide which yarns to use for a project. The choice available these days is quite stunning and ranges from naturals to synthetics, alpaca, metallic, cashmere, silk, acrylic, and blends of wool, to name but a few.

Yarns come in different thicknesses or weights. Fine yarns—such as two- and three-ply, for instance—are normally used for baby garments and shawls. Probably the most widely used yarns are four-ply and double-knitting weight. Then we come to Aran and chunky weight yarns that knit up quickly and produce heavyweight garments. All the projects in this book have specified yarns, but you can substitute these for different yarns as long as you check your gauge before

What Yarn Should You Use?

Throughout this book, I've noted the yarns that I used to make the samples, but don't feel wedded to those exact yarns unless you want to recreate the knits exactly as they appear in the photos. Here are a few things to take into account:

- **Superwash.** Eventually, the lucky baby who receives your handmade gift is going to spit up on it—or worse. I can't stress this enough: make sure to choose a yarn that can be put through the washing machine. Extra points if it can go through the dryer, too. After all, new parents may spend more time doing laundry than they do sleeping.
- **Softness.** Feel the yarn before you buy it. Babies have sensitive skin!
- **Baby Friendliness.** Some major yarn brands make lines specifically for babies. You don't *have* to go with one of these, but if you're feeling nervous, these are a safe bet—and there are some lovely options available.
- **Color.** Pastels are sweet and neutrals are in, but did you know that very tiny babies prefer high-contrast patterns? That's why they're so attracted to black-and-white toys and bright primary colors: their brains are learning to distinguish colors. So if you feel like going bold, go bold!

beginning the work and you keep to the same ply or weight recommended in the pattern. If you do decide to change yarns, then it is possible that you will achieve a different look in your finished garment than that of the design shown.

ACCESSORIES

Before embarking on your first garment, you need to acquire a few basic tools. There are a ton of knitting accessories available, so here are some of the basics to get you started.

Needles

There are many brands of knitting needles available these days, and the price range is varied. It is wise to invest in some good-quality needles, since these will give you many years of service, but sometimes price might be a big deciding factor for you. The type of material you choose is really up to your personal preference and budget.

WOOD

Wooden needles are a very popular, high-quality choice. Wooden needles offer knitters more flexibility while working. They will more readily conform to the movements of your hands than other materials, like metal. Because of this, knitters with hands that need a more forgiving material should take this into consideration.

Keep in mind that since wood is a natural material, you will also need to factor in the maintenance they require. From time to time, you will need to wax or oil your needles to keep them in good condition. They should also be stored in any area with low-moisture since wood tends to expand in high humidity.

Price should also be a factor in deciding the type of wood you choose. Depending on the species of wood, wood needles can get fairly pricey. If you still want the warmth and smoothness that wood offers—but don't want to spend as much—bamboo is a great alternative.

Another thing to consider is for those that want to show off their finished products online. Wooden needles photograph beautifully and

Wooden needles

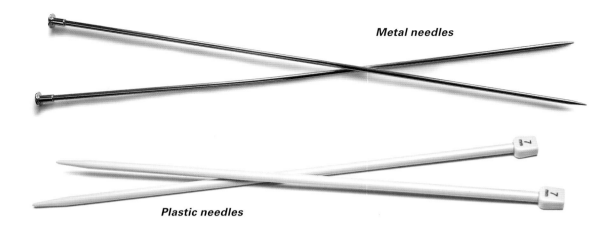

Metal needles

Plastic needles

will add warmth to photos when used as props. You'll easily enhance your work and have your friends and family crooning over its beauty for sure.

METAL

Metal needles are widely available online and at local craft retailers. They come in many different material types: aluminum, stainless steel, nickel, brass, etc. Though not as flexible as wooden needles—and not as easy on the hands—metal needles are guaranteed to offer knitters smooth surfaces. This will allow you to knit with speed, and you'll find your stitches gliding easily from needle to needle quicker than thought possible.

When compared to wood, metal also offers less maintenance and more strength. Strength is a feature that comes in handy when creating larger, heavier pieces. Though most of the projects in this book are rather small, it's something to consider for future projects you might do.

PLASTIC

Plastic needles are almost like a combination of wood and metal when considering the pros and cons. If you want the flexibility and warmth of wooden needles without the required upkeep, plastic is an excellent option. This type is a favorite among those with joint pain in their hands.

When considering smoothness, plastic needles are generally less grabby than most wood needles. When compared to metal, however, plastic doesn't offer as much smoothness or speed, but they are much lighter. Plastic also isn't as durable as metal, so would not be a good choice when working with larger projects or heavier yarns.

Beginner knitters might want to consider purchasing plastic first since they are the cheapest option available.

Additional Essential Accessories

A tape measure, stitch holders, crochet hooks, row markers, a cable needle, a good, sharp pair of needlework scissors, and a range of sewing needles are recommended, too. A knitting bag is also a very handy thing in which to store your work in progress; not only does it keep your work clean while you are knitting, but you can also store the patterns and yarns you are using all in one place, ready to begin work at a moment's notice.

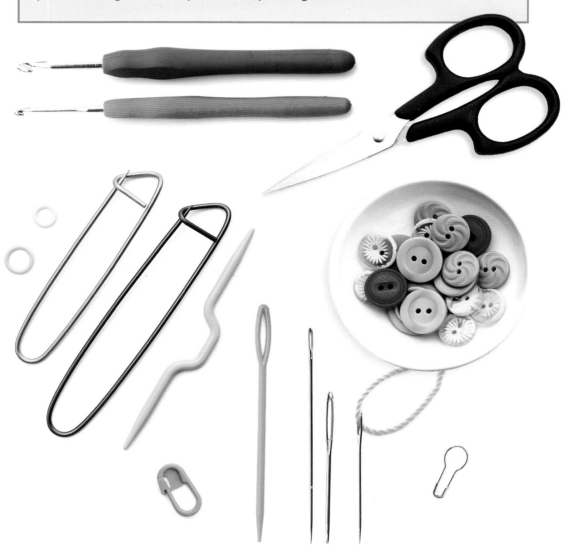

Techniques

CASTING ON AND BINDING OFF

There are several methods for casting on and binding off. Some knitting patterns will stipulate a particular method, depending on the effect required within the pattern—it is common to bind off in pattern, for instance. Make sure that your cast on and bind off stitches remain elastic by either working them reasonably loosely or using a larger size needle than stated if you think you work very tightly. Most patterns will tell you which side of the knitting to finish your work on, but as a general rule, most binding off is done with the right side of the work facing.

Creating a Slip Knot

Before starting any knitting project, you'll need to create a slip knot. To start, unwind some yarn to cast on (ideally, as much yarn as the pattern requires for casting on). Make a slip knot by creating a loop about 4 in. (10cm) from the end of your yarn, then twist the loop once in a clockwise direction. Reach through with your fingers, pull the right-hand strand up through the loop, and tighten. Proceed with one of the two following casting methods.

Casting On—Two-Needle Method

This method involves creating a row of loops cast on to a needle. The second needle is used to build a series of inter-joining loops in a row. Hold the needle with the stitches in your left hand and the needle to make the stitches in your right hand. (If you are left-handed, do the reverse.)

1. Make a slip knot and place it onto the left-hand needle. Then insert the right-hand needle through the front loop as if you were making a knit stitch. Pass the yarn under and over the point of the right-hand needle (again, as if you were making a knit stitch).

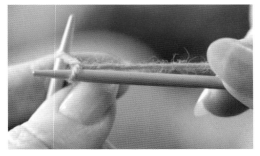

2. Using the right-hand needle, draw the yarn through the slip knot to form a new stitch.

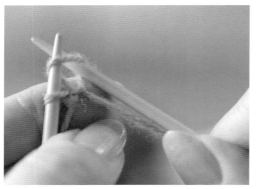

3. Transfer the new stitch to left-hand needle, insert the right-hand needle through the front of the new stitch, and repeat steps 1 and 2.

4. Continue in this way until you have casted on the required number of stitches specified in your pattern.

Casting On—One-Needle or Thumb Method

1. Make a slip knot and place it on the needle.

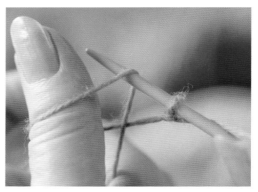

2. Wind the yarn clockwise around your thumb and hold firmly. Insert the point of the needle through the loop on your thumb.

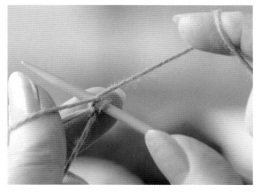

3. Wind the yarn in your left hand around the back of the point of the needle and in between the needle and your thumb. Pull the point of the needle under the yarn to form a stitch.

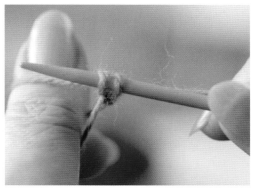

4. Slip the stitch on to the needle close to the slip knot. Continue in this way until you have the required number of stitches specified in your pattern.

Binding Off

The technique of binding off is used to provide the finished edge to the end of your work. It is also used when you shape pieces of work or make buttonholes. It is usual to bind off on the right side of your work; however, follow the instructions since you may have to bind off in pattern. Don't pull stitches too tightly when binding off; this may result in a puckered edge or make it difficult when sewing the seams of the garment together.

1. Work the first two stitches in pattern. With the yarn at the back of the work, insert the point of the needle through the first stitch.

2. Using the left-hand needle, lift the first stitch over the second stitch and then off the needle.

3. Work the next stitch in pattern. Once again using the left-hand needle, lift the first stitch over the second stitch and off the needle.

4. Continue to follow step 3 all the way along the row until you're left with a single stitch. Slip this last stitch off the needle and firmly pull the end of the yarn through it to secure.

KNIT STITCH

To create any fabric when beginning to knit, there are a couple of fundamental stitches you can learn. For the projects in this book, however, the knit stitch is the only one that you need to master. The knit stitch is the first you would normally learn when beginning to knit; this forms a ridged fabric known as garter stitch. Every project in this book uses only this stitch. Follow the steps in one of the two methods below to create the knit stitch.

The English/American Method

In this method, you use your right hand to pull the yarn around the right needle. You control the amount of yarn used with each stitch is controlled by winding your working yarn between your last two fingers. Your left hand moves the knitting forward while your right hand makes the stitch, lifting the yarn, placing it over the needle, and pulling it through the loop.

1. Holding the needle with the cast-on stitches in your left hand, wind the yarn around the little finger of your right hand, under the next two fingers and over the top of your index finger.

2. Keeping the yarn at the back of the work, hold the second needle in your right hand and insert it into the front of the first stitch.

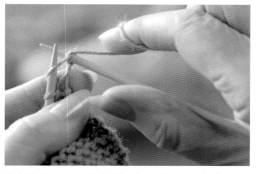

3. With your right index finger, bring the yarn forward, under and over the point of the right-hand needle.

4. Pull the yarn through the loop and push the resulting stitch toward the point of the left-hand needle.

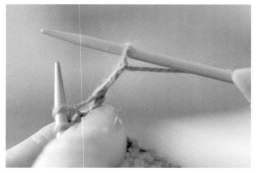

5. Slip it off onto the right-hand needle. Repeat the process until you have the required number of knit stitches.

The Continental Method

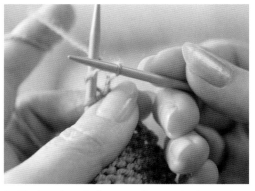

1. Hold the needle with cast-on stitches in your right hand, wind the yarn over your left index finger, and lay it across the palm of your hand. Then take up the slack between your two last fingers.

3. Twist the right needle and place the point under the working yarn to pull the loop onto the right-hand needle.

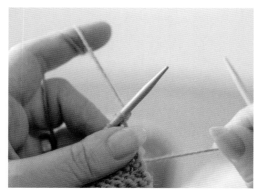

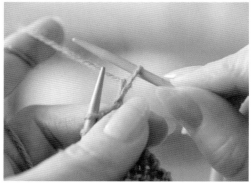

2. Place the work in your left hand. Extend your left index finger, pulling yarn behind the needle. Use your left thumb and middle finger to push the first stitch toward the point, and insert the right-hand needle.

4. It may help to hold the loop with your right index finger while you pull it down through the stitch. Pull the new stitch onto the right-hand needle, and repeat the process until you have the required number of knit stitches.

Increasing and Decreasing

When working on some projects, it is necessary to shape the pieces as you work. In order to do this, you will need to lose or gain stitches on the rows as you knit. This is done by either increasing the number of stitches (done by knitting twice into the same stitch) or decreasing (achieved by knitting two stitches together). There are quite a few ways of doing this, but most patterns will state clearly which method is recommended.

Increase

There are also two kinds of increases used in some of the patterns contained in this book. It's really important to use the increase as stated in the project. If you use the wrong increase method then the stitch counts will not work out. It should also be noted that adding increases on one side will result in giving your project a slanted look.

- kfb = This means that you will knit into the front and back of the designated stitch. This easy stitch will essentially turn one stitch into two, and is a very common stitch to use when knitting.
- m1 = This stitch indicates that you should "make one." To do so, pick up and knit the horizontal strand of yarn between the stitch just knitted and the next stitch, and knit into the back of it. It's a great stitch to use when you want to increase

more discretely. Be aware, though; this stitch can be a little tricky, so practice it a few times before you attempt to use it for real.

Decrease

To decrease you will need to knit two stitches together. As you work through the projects in this book, you may come across a couple of different decreasing abbreviations.

- k2tog = This means to knit two stitches together. This is the most basic way to increase and will slant the stitches to the right.
- k2togtbl = This abbreviation means that you will need to knit two stitches together through the back loops of the stitches. Doing this slants the decrease to the left, while also adding a decorative twist to your piece at the same time.

MEASUREMENTS AND MEASURING

Most of the garments within this book are designed with an allowance for comfortable fit. When measuring pieces of knitting while working on your project, it is much easier and more reliable to count the number of rows you have knitted. Sleeves and side seams will all fit so much better if the rows are the same. Sewing in sleeves sometimes causes problems, but if you pin and ease the sleeve in place before stitching, you should get a good result. Raglan sleeves are easier to stitch in since they lay flat when sewing.

It's important to note that when a range of sizes is given, the number of stitches will change. For example, a pattern may indicate that it's for chest sizes of 16¼ [18, 20, 22, 24] in. (41 [46, 51, 56, 61] cm). The smaller size is given first before the bracket, and the larger sizes are given in ascending order inside the brackets. As you go through the pattern, you'll find directions such as "cast on 26 [28, 31, 33, 36] sts." This means that for the 16¼ in. (41cm) size, you will be casting on 26 stitches; for 18 in. (46cm), you'll be casting on 28 stitches; for 20 in. (51cm), you'll be casting on 31 stitches; and so on.

Measurements in this book are given in both inches (imperial) and metric. Please choose one and stick with it throughout the project.

Gauge

Gauge is very often overlooked and can have a detrimental effect to your finished garments. Always check your gauge before you begin working, changing needle sizes to obtain the stated stitch count if needed. If you get fewer stitches to the inch (centimeter) than stated, your gauge is too loose and a smaller needle is required. If

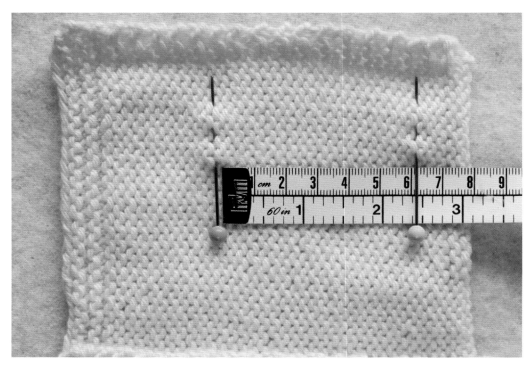

you get more stitches to the inch (centimeter) than stated, your gauge is too tight and a larger needle will be required. When measuring your gauge, don't stretch the work out or squish it up to make it fit; knit up one or two samples until you get it just right.

PICKING UP STITCHES

Some of the designs in the book have neckbands and front bands knitted on to them, which entails picking up stitches along an already knitted edge. Many knitters hate picking up stitches; it takes a lot of practice to perfect the technique, but here are a few ideas to help.

- Use a smaller size needle than the one you are going to continue with to make the process easier.
- Do not pick up stitches at the very edge of the knitting; picking up the stitches that lie one stitch in from the edge will result in a much neater finish.
- Always try to ensure that stitches are picked up evenly along the edge or neckband when working.
- Always pick up the amount of stitches recommended, and make sure they are even on both sides of the neck and front.
- When working with cardigans, measure the length of the fronts, then divide the amount of stitches you need to pick up into the length. This will allow you to end up with

a neat, even button or buttonhole band that sits flat.
- Work through the same stitch all the way up the fronts.

1. Hold the working yarn behind the completed piece. Insert the needle through it, between the rows and between the last two stitches of each row, from front to back.

2. Wind the yarn over the needle as if you were going to knit a stitch, then pull a loop of yarn through to form a stitch. Continue until the required number of stitches is formed.

JOINING NEW YARNS

Sometimes you will need to add new yarn into your piece, such as when you run out of yarn or a new color is needed. It's advisable to join new yarn at the beginning of a row. Unless dictated by the pattern, try not to join new yarn in in the middle of a row—it makes for an uneven bump in the fabric and can result in a hole if the ends work loose.

Working with Two or More Colors

A couple of the designs in the book use more than one color in a row. When working these, it is advisable to use the stranding method whereby you carry the yarn not in use fairly loosely across the back of the work as you knit. The yarn can be tied into the work on every third of fourth stitch to keep the work neat and elastic. Care must be taken not to pull yarn too tightly when doing this; otherwise, it will result in puckering of the fabric.

Adding New Yarn at the Beginning of a Row

1. Insert the right-hand needle into the first stitch on the left-hand need and wind both old and new yarns over it. Knit the stitch with both yarns.

2. Drop the old yarn and pick up the new, then knit the next two stitches with the short end and the working yarn.

3. Drop the short end of the new yarn and continue knitting in pattern.

4. On the subsequent row, purl (reversed knit stitch) the three double stitches normally.

Adding a New Color within a Row

1. With old yarn at the back of the work, insert the point of the right needle into the stitch. Wind the new yarn over the needle and use it as your new stitch.

2. Knit the next two stitches with both of the new and old colors.

3. Drop the short end and continue knitting with the new yarn while carrying the old yarn across the back. On subsequent rows, purl (reversed knit stich) the double stitches normally.

MAKING A TWISTED CORD

Take two lengths of yarn and fold into a double strand. To measure the amount you need, keep in mind that when folded and twisted your original length will end up a quarter of its length. Tie a knot in each end of yarn, insert a pencil in one end and secure the other to a doorknob. Twist the pencil until the yarn is tightly twisted, keeping it taut at all times. Fold yarn in half and let it twist on itself, then even it out and tie the other end firmly to prevent it from untwisting.

FINISHING STITCHES

After completing the knitting portion of your work of art, you will need to add the final stitches. Always read the ball band of the yarn you have used, since this will give you details about pressing and washing your garment.

When finishing with garter stitch, it is much easier to have the right sides of the work facing you and to catch the little bobbles on the row ends together, matching row for row, which will give an almost invisible seam.

Sewing with a backstitch isn't really recommended for the garter stitch, since the resulting seam will be quite bulky.

Sewing the pieces together is sometimes daunting to novice knitters, but if you work methodically and carefully, you will find it is quite simple. Take care to stretch front bands slightly when sewing them on, as this gives a firmer and more professional finish to cardigans. Most patterns will give instructions on assembling a particular garment for you to follow.

CORRECTING MISTAKES

It is inevitable that you will make the occasional mistake in your work. Checking back at regular intervals is always a good plan—should the need arise to correct errors, there will not be too many rows to unpick. A dropped stitch can often be picked up with the aid of a crochet hook and worked back up the piece of knitting one row at a time. If you need to unravel work, do it slowly and carefully, using a smaller size needle to pick up the stitches from the unraveled row, and change back to the correct size needle to begin working again.

AVOIDING ISSUES

We all have problems from time to time when things we are making just don't go right. It can be very frustrating, especially after you have spent quite a lot of money on yarns to make the project. Here are a few little tips to help you before starting your project.

- Every pattern you buy will have been tested by a pattern checker. The yarns used for the project are yarns made specifically by the pattern manufacturer. The gauge has been worked out to accommodate the yarns stated. If you buy a substitute yarn, then it is vital you check the gauge against the gauge recommended in the pattern. Just because your substitute yarn is the same weight doesn't guarantee the gauge will work out the same. Don't be afraid to change your needle size to obtain the right amount of stitches to the inch (centimeter).

- The yardage can also differ quite a lot, so check the yardage on the yarn you buy against that of the recommended yarn. Buying an extra couple of balls is always a good plan. There's nothing worse than nearing the end of your garment and running out of yarn!
- Check dye lots on all the ball bands. Most good yarn stores will do this for you anyway, but it is always best to double check. Colors can vary quite a lot in different dye batches.
- Don't rely on measuring alone for lengths of side seams, sleeve seams, and so on. Tedious though it may be, counting the rows on your pieces will ensure that everything fits together perfectly when assembling your garment.
- As you knit, wind off a few yards (centimeters) at a time. Do this to check for knots or spinning faults. I can't count the number of times I have been knitting away and found a rogue knot just a short distance from the end of the row and had to pull the whole row back and start again.

Conversion Charts and Abbreviations

NEEDLE SIZE CONVERSION CHART

Metric sizes	US sizes	UK sizes
2.00mm	0	14
2.25mm	1	13
2.75mm	2	12
3.00mm	–	11
3.25mm	3	10
3.50mm	4	–
3.75mm	5	9
4.00mm	6	8
4.50mm	7	7
5.00mm	8	6
5.50mm	9	5
6.00mm	10	4
6.50mm	10½	3
7.00mm	–	2
7.50mm	–	1
8.00mm	11	0
9.00mm	13	00
10.00mm	15	000
12.00mm	17	–
16.00mm	19	–
19.00mm	35	–
25.00mm	50	–

US TO UK TO AUSTRALIAN YARN WEIGHT CONVERSIONS

US	UK	Australia
Lace weight	1 ply	2 ply
Fingering	2 ply	3 ply
Super fine	3 ply	3 ply
Fine	4 ply	5 ply
Light/DK	DK	8 ply
Medium/Aran	Aran	10 ply
Bulky/chunky	Chunky	12 ply
Super bulky/chunky	Super chunky	14 ply

ABBREVIATIONS

alt	alternate
approx.	approximately
beg	beginning
cm	centimeters
dec	decrease
foll	following
garter stitch	knit every row knit
inc	increase
k	knit
kfb	knit into the front and back of the stitch
patt	pattern
psso	pass slipped stitch over
rem	remaining
rep(s)	repeat(s)
RS	right side
skp	slip one stitch, knit one stitch, pass slipped stitch over
sl1	slip one stitch
sl st	slipped stitch
st	stitch
tog	together
WS	wrong side
yfwd	yarn forward over needle to make a hole

US TO UK TERMINOLOGY

US	UK
Gauge	Tension
Bind off	Cast off

Projects

Geometric Blanket

This pretty blanket is simple and speedy to make. Using super-soft chunky yarns and big needles, you will need to make just 12 squares. The edgings are worked separately and sewn onto the blanket. I used very bright colors, one plain and one with random shades. The way the squares are sewn together forms a geometric pattern. You can follow my idea or place squares to create your own design.

Materials

- King Cole Comfort Chunky Yarn, 116 yds. (106m) US bulky
  - 3 x 100g balls in shade 1967 Laguna (yarn A)
  - 3 x 100g balls white/multi in shade 492 Pavlova (yarn B)
- Knitting needles size 5.50mm (US 9, UK 5)
- Large-eyed sewing needle

. . . .

Gauge: 12 sts x 14 rows measures 4 in. (10cm)
using 5.50mm (US 9 UK 5) needles

Measurements: One square measures 7 in. (17cm).
You will need to make 12 squares. The complete
size is 24 in. wide x 31 in. long (61 x 79cm).

Abbreviations: See page 27

To Make a Square

Using 5.50mm (US 9, UK 5) needles
  and yarn A, cast on 2 sts.
Next Row: Inc in first st, k1.
Next Row: K3.
Next Row: Sl1, inc, k1.
Next Row: Sl1 inc, k to end.
Rep last row to 30 sts.
Change to yarn B.
Next Row: Sl1, k2tog, k to end.
Rep last row until 3 sts rem.
Next Row: Sl1, k2tog.
Next Row: K2tog and fasten off.
Make 11 more squares.

Edging (made in 4 strips; 2 x blue and 2 x multi)

SHORT EDGES

Using yarn A, cast on 2 sts.
Next Row: K2.
Next Row: Inc in first st, k1.
Next Row: K3.
Next Row: Inc in first st, k to end.
Next Row: K4.
Continue to inc at the same edge until
  you have 8 sts.
Now continue on these sts until piece,
  when slightly stretched, fits along
  short edge of blanket.

SHAPE MITERED CORNER AS FOLLOWS

Next Row: K2tog, k to end.
Next Row: Knit.

Rep last 2 rows until 2 sts rem.
Next Row: K2tog and fasten off.

Long Edges (make 2 alike)
Work as short edges but use B.

Finishing
Work in all ends neatly. Assemble squares in four rows of three. Refer to diagram for placement of squares and side edgings. Now join the strips to form the blanket.

Sew edging to sides of blanket, sewing the mitered corners together.

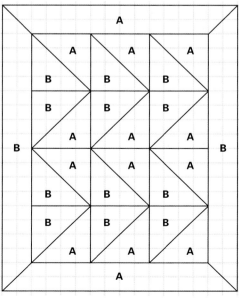

Easy Burp Cloth

A perfect project for the novice knitter, this useful burp cloth can be made very quickly. The raised pattern is simply a slipped stitch on the right side of the work that gives texture to the fabric. I used a cotton yarn so that the project will wash well.

Materials

- ✕ 1 x 50g ball Rico Baby Cotton Soft DK (worsted weight) in shade 32 Emerald, 137 yds. (125m)
- ✕ Knitting needles size 3.75mm (US 4, UK 9)

Gauge: Not critical on this project
Measurements: 7½ in. wide x 13½ in. long (19 x 34cm)
Abbreviations: See page 27

Instructions

Using 3.75mm (US 4, UK 9) needles,
cast on 2 sts.

Next Row: K1, kfb, k to end.

Rep last row until you have 43 sts on
the needles.

BEGIN PATTERN

Row 1: * K3, sl1, rep from * to last 3
sts, k3.

Row 2: Knit.

Continue in pattern as on last 2 rows
until work measures 6 in. (15cm),
ending on a Row 2.

Next Row: K1, k2tog, k to end of row.

Rep last row until 3 sts rem on needle.

Next Row: K2tog, k1.

Next Row: K2tog and fasten off.

This project is reversible. The back is simpler, but still pretty.

Tickled Pink Bootie and Headband Set

Novice knitters will find this sweet set very simple to make. The addition of a slipped stitch on one row adds a little bit of pattern interest to the headband. I used a pink-flecked yarn, but you can choose a color to suit your own tastes. Knit the bow in a contrasting shade to make your headband look even cuter!

Materials

- ✻ 1 [2] x 50g ball Sirdar Snuggly DK (worsted weight) in shade 267 Strawberry Mousse, approx. 179 yds. (165m)
- ✻ Knitting needles size 4.00mm (US 6, UK 8)
- ✻ Large-eyed sewing needle

....

Gauge: 20 sts x 40 rows measures 4 in. (10cm) using 4.00mm (US 6, UK 8) needles

Measurements: To fit ages 0–3 months (3–6 months)

Abbreviations: See page 27

Headband

Using 4.00mm (US 6, UK 8) needles,
cast on 11 sts.
Next Row: Knit.
Next Row: K5, sl1, k5.
Next Row: Knit.
Rep last 2 rows for 12 in. (30cm)
[13¼ in. (34cm)], ending on a k row.
Bind off.

Bow

Using 4.00mm (US 6, UK 8) needles,
cast on 9 sts.
Next Row: Knit.
Next Row (RS): K2, sl1, k3, sl1, k2.
Next Row: Knit.
Rep the last 2 rows until the work
measures 6¼ in. (16cm), ending on a
knit row. Bind off.

Booties

You will begin at the base of
the bootie.
Using 4.00mm (US 6, UK 8) needles,
cast on 36 [40] sts.
Work 12 [14] rows in garter stitch
(every row knit).

NOW BEGIN TO SHAPE THE TOE

Next Row: K15 [17], k2tog, k2, skp, k15
[17].
Next Row: Knit.
Next Row: K14 [16], k2tog, k2, skp, K14
[16].
Next Row: K13 [15], k2tog, k2, skp, k13
[15].
Next Row: K12 [14], k2tog, k2, skp, k12
[14].

Next Row: K11 [13], k2tog, k2, skp, k11 [13].

Next Row: K10 [12], k2tog, k2, skp, k10 [12].

Work straight without further decs for 16 [20] rows.

Bind off fairly loosely. Make another bootie to match.

Finishing

BOOTIE

Fold the piece in half and sew the seam on the base of the foot and back leg. Fold over the top to form a cuff.

HEADBAND

Sew the short seam on the headband with a neat flat seam. Sew the short seam on the bow, folding so that the seam is at the back of the bow. Thread a needle with some matching yarn and run a gathering thread through the center of the piece. Draw up firmly to form a bow shape, securing with a few stitches. Sew the bow onto the headband.

Bunny Earflap Hat

Knit this cute bunny ears hat in just a couple of evenings. Although I have used a darker shade, any number of pastel shade like pinks, greens, or yellows would look just as sweet. This is a very simple and quick project and one any novice could try their hand at.

Materials

- 1 x 100g ball King Cole Comfort DK (worsted weight) in shade 3277 Truffle, 340 yds. (310m)
- Knitting needles size 3.25mm (US 3, UK 10)
- Large-eyed sewing needle

Gauge: 21 sts x 40 rows measures 4 in. (10 cm) using 3.25mm (US 3, UK 10) needles

Measurements: To fit 6–12 months. Hat circumference approx. 15 in. (38cm)

Abbreviations: See page 27

Hat

BEGIN WITH EARFLAPS (MAKE 2)

Using 3.25mm (US 3, UK 10) needles, cast on 2 sts.

Next Row: Knit.
Next Row: Kfb in next st, k1 (3 sts).
Next Row: Knit.
Next Row: K1, kfb, k to end.
Rep last row until there are 19 sts on the needle.
Knit 2 rows straight and leave on a holder.
Work another piece to match.

WORK MAIN PART OF HAT

Using 3.25mm (US 3, UK 10) needles, cast on 9 sts, k across 19 sts from one earflap, cast on 32 sts, k across 19 sts of other earflap, cast on 9 sts (88 sts).

Continue in garter stitch until work measures 4 in. (10cm) from start of main piece.

SHAPE CROWN OF HAT

Row 1: * K6, k2tog, rep from * to end.
Row 2 and foll alt (even-numbered) rows: Knit.
Row 3: * K5, k2tog, rep from * to end.

Row 5: * K4, k2tog, rep from * to end.
Row 7: * K3, k2tog, rep from * to end.
Row 9: * K2, k2tog, rep from * to end.
Row 11: * K1, k2tog, rep from * to end.
Row 13: * K2tog, rep from * to end.
Row 14: * K2tog, rep from * to last st, k1.
Break yarn and thread through rem sts on needle. Draw up and fasten off securely.

Ears (make 2)

Using 3.25mm (US 3, UK 10) needles, cast on 2 sts.
Next Row: Knit.
Next Row: Kfb, k1 (3 sts).

Next Row: Knit.
Next Row: K1, kfb in next st, k to end.
Rep last row until there are 16 sts on the needle.
Continue on these sts in garter stitch for 44 more rows.
Next Row: K2tog, across row.
Next Row: K2tog, across row. Draw thread through rem sts and pull up tight, secure, and fasten off.

Finishing

Sew seam of hat that runs down center back. Pleat top of ear and sew to crown of hat. Repeat with the other ear.

T-Shaped Sweater and Simple Shoes

This is a super simple T-shaped top for a baby. It's perfect for the novice knitter, and, with the use of different colors and turned-back cuffs, the project looks anything but simple. Pretty little shoes complete the outfit.

Materials

- 2 [2, 3] x 50g balls Sirdar Snuggly Doodle DK w(worsted weight) in shade 202 Chatterbox (yarn A)
- 2 [2, 3] x 50g balls Sirdar Snuggly DK (worsted weight) in shade 482 Bubbles Blue (yarn B)
- Knitting needles size 4.00mm (US 6, UK 8) and 3.25mm (US 3, UK 10)
- Large-eyed sewing needle
- 4 buttons

. . . .

Gauge: 20 sts x 40 rows measures 4 in. (10cm) using 4.00mm (US 6, UK 8) needles

Measurements: To fit chest size 16 [18, 20] in. (41 [46, 51] cm]). Length from back neck to hem 10 [11, 12] in. (25 [29, 31] cm). Sleeve length without cuff turned back 6 [7, 8] in. (15 [17, 20] cm).

Abbreviations: See page 27

Special Abbreviation: m1 = pick up the horizontal strand of yarn between the stitch just knitted and the next stitch on the needle, and knit into the back of it, thus increasing one stitch

Back and Front Alike

NOTE: First row is RS of work.

Using 4.00mm (US 6, UK 8) needles and yarn A, cast on 42 [47, 52] sts.

Work in garter stitch for 4 [6, 7¾] in. (10 [15, 20] cm).

Change to yarn B and continue until work measures 7¾ [9¾, 11¾] in. (20 [25, 30] cm), ending on a WS row.

Change to A and work 4 rows in garter stitch.

Bind off.

Sleeves (make 2 alike)

Using 4.00mm (US 6, UK 8) needles and B, cast on 38 [41, 50] sts.

Knit 2 rows.

Change to A and work in garter stitch for 4¾ [6, 7¾] in. (12 [15, 20] cm).

Bind off.

Shoes (make 2 alike to fit one size/3 months)

Using 3.25mm (US 3, UK 10) needles and A, cast on 33 sts.

Next Row: Knit.

Next Row: K1, m1, k15, m1, k1, m1, k15, m1, k1 (37 sts).

Next Row: Knit.
Next Row: K2, m1, k15, m1, k3, m1, k15, m1, k2 (41 sts).
Next Row: Knit.
Next Row: K3, m1, k15, m1, k5, m1, k15, m1, k3 (45 sts).
Next Row: Knit.
Next Row: K4, m1, k15, m1, k7, m1, k15, m1, k4 (49 sts).
Change to B and work 15 rows in garter stitch.
Change to A.
Next Row: K16, (skp) 4 times, k1, (k2tog) 4 times, k16 (41 sts).
Next Row: Knit.
Bind off.

Straps (make 2 alike)

Using 3.25mm (US 3, UK 10) needles and B, cast on 5 sts. Work 25 rows in garter stitch.

Next Row: Make buttonhole. K2, yfwd, k2tog, k2.
Work 2 more rows in garter stitch and bind off.

Button Loops (make 2)

Using 3.25mm (US 3, UK 10) needles and B, cast on 12 sts. Bind off.

Finishing

Work in ends neatly on all pieces. Overlap front and back neck for 2 in. (5cm) on each side to form "envelope neck." Sew button loops onto front neck on either side. Sew on buttons to correspond with loops. Take sleeves and fold in half lengthways. Mark center point of fold. Match this point to shoulder seam of back and front. Sew sleeve in place to back and front. Repeat with other sleeve. Join sleeve and side seams. Turn back cuffs on sleeves.

Sew back seam and sole of shoes. Sew straps to side of shoes, remembering to reverse for second strap. Sew on buttons to correspond with buttonholes.

Simple Pom-Pom Hat

This is the perfect project for the novice knitter.
The end result is the cutest little hat! Add two
big pom-poms to complete the look.

Materials

- 1 x 100g ball King Cole Comfort Multi Chunky
  Yarn in shade 492 Pavlova (yarn A)
- Small amounts of King Cole Comfort Chunky
  Yarn in shade 1967 Laguna (yarn B)
- Knitting needles size 5.50mm (US 9, UK 5)
- Large-eyed sewing needle
- Pom-pom maker

. . . .

Gauge: 14 sts x 28 rows measures 4 in. (10cm)
using 5.50mm (US 9, UK 5) needles

Measurements: To fit ages 6–12 months;
15 in. (38cm) circumference

Abbreviations: See page 27

Instructions

Using 5.50mm (US 9, UK 5) needles
and yarn A, cast on 27 sts.
Row 1 (RS): * K3, sl1, rep from * to
last 3 sts, k3.
Next Row: Knit.
Rep last 2 rows for 12 in. (30cm),
ending on a Row 1.
Bind off.

Finishing

Fold piece in half. Sew the side
seams. Using yarn B, make two large
pom-poms. Attach securely to each
side of the top of the hat.

Color-Block Hooded Scarf

This hooded scarf is a very simple project. Knitted on big needles and using an Aran weight yarn, it doesn't take long to complete. You just need to be able to increase and decrease stitches. The yarn is a graded yarn choice, but you can use any similar weight yarn you like.

Materials

- ✄ 1 x 100g ball of Caron Baby Cakes Yarn in Aran weight (Fisherman or Medium) in shade 50015 Fresh Air
- ✄ Knitting needles size 4.50mm (US 7, UK 7)
- ✄ Large-eyed sewing needle
- ✄ Pom-pom maker

Gauge: 17 sts x 32 rows measures 4 in. (10cm) using 4.50mm (US 7, UK 7) needles

Measurements: 14¼ in. (34cm) from point to point

Abbreviations: See page 27

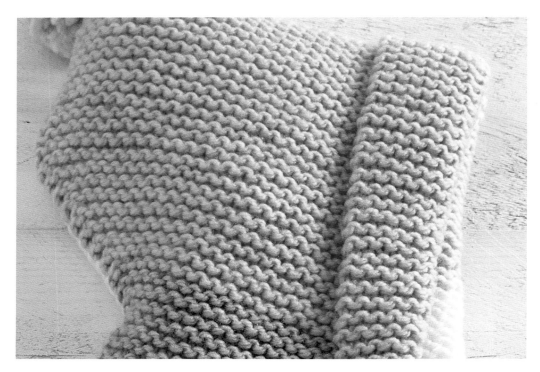

Instructions

Using 4.50mm (US 7, UK 7) needles, cast on 2 sts.

Row 1: Knit.

Row 2: Kfb in first and last st (4 sts).

Next Row: Knit.

Next Row: Kfb in first st, k2, kfb in last st (6 sts).

Next Row: Knit.

Next Row: K1, kfb in next stitch, k to end.

Rep the last row until you have 26 sts on the needles.

Work in garter stitch for 11 in. (28cm).

BEGIN TO INCREASE FOR HOOD

Row 1: K to last 2 sts, kfb, k1. Place marker at the end of this row to denote the beginning of the hood.

Row 2: Knit.

Inc as on last 2 rows until you have 38 sts on the needles.

Continue in garter stitch until work measures 9½ in. (24cm) from last row, ending on a Row 2.

DECREASE AS FOLLOWS

Next Row: K to last 3 sts, k2tog, k1. Mark this row as end of hood.

Next Row: Knit.

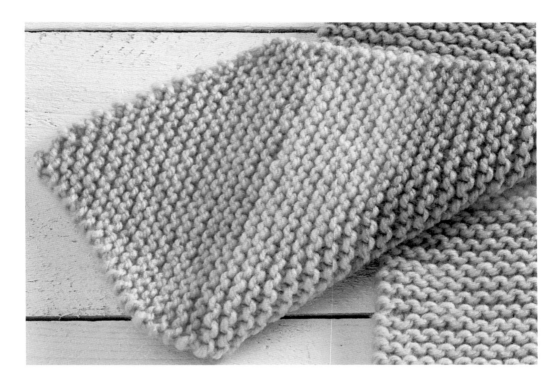

Continue as on last 2 rows until 26 sts
   rem on the needles.
Work in garter stitch until work
   measures 11 in. (28cm) from
   last row.

DECREASE FOR POINT

Next row: K1, k2tog, knit to end.
Rep last row until 3 sts rem.
Next Row: K3tog. Fasten off.
Join hood from marker to marker. Fold
   back brim and secure in place. Make
   a pom-pom and sew firmly to back
   of the hood.

Navy and Speckle Striped Booties

These little booties are quite easy to make as they are worked from the sole upward. There is no picking up of stitches at the instep, either, as they are decreased in rows instead. I have added a contrasting turned-back cuff to add a bit more interest and make them extra warm for tiny feet. You can use a contrasting yarn as I have, or you can work the complete bootie in just one shade.

Materials

- ✄ Sirdar Snuggly DK Yarn (worsted weight), 179 yds. (165m)
  - 1 x 50g ball in shade 224 Light Navy (yarn A)
  - 1 x 50g ball in shade 707 Polka Dot (yarn B)
- ✄ Knitting needles sizes 3.25mm (US 3, UK 10) and 3.75mm (US 5, UK 9)
- ✄ Large-eyed sewing needle

....

Gauge: 22 sts x 40 rows measures 4 in. (10cm) using 3.75mm (US 5, UK 9) needles

Measurements: To fit ages 3–6 months. Sole measures approx. 3 in. (8cm)

Abbreviations: See page 27

Special Abbreviations: m1 = pick up the horizontal strand of yarn between the stitch just knitted and the next stitch on the needle, and knit into the back of it, thus increasing one stitch; k2togtbl = knit 2 stitches together through the back loops

Booties (make 2 alike)

Using 3.75mm (US 5, UK 9) needles
  and yarn A, cast on 27 sts.
Knit 1 row.

Row 1: K2, m1, k11, m1, k1, m1, k11,
  m1, k2 (31 sts).

Row 2: Knit.

Row 3: K2, m1, k12, m1, k3, m1, k12,
  m1, k2.

Row 4: Knit.

Row 5: K2, m1, k13, m1, k5, m1, k13,
  m1, k2.

Row 6: Knit.

Row 7: K2, m1, k14, m1, k7, m1, k14, m1, k2.

Row 8: Knit.

Join B.

Rows 9–10: K2 rows B.

Rows 11–12: K2 rows A.

Rows 13–24: Rep Rows 9–12 3 more times.

Break B and continue in A.

SHAPE INSTEP AS FOLLOWS

Next Row: K26, turn.

Next Row: K9, turn.

Next Row: K8, k2tog, turn.

Next Row: K8, k2togtbl, turn.

Rep last 2 rows 5 more times. Turn.

Next Row: K9, k across rem sts on the left-hand needle.

Next Row: K across all sts.

Change to B and 3.25mm (US 3, UK 10) needles. Work 14 more rows in garter stitch.

Knit 16 rows.

Change to A and knit 1 row. Bind off.

Finishing

Sew seam on back and leg of bootie. Make a twisted tie with yarn A and thread through the fabric at the ankle of bootie. Tie at front in a bow.

Pink Ombré Baby Bib

This pretty bib will need a little more concentration when increasing and decreasing, but the main part of the project uses a garter stitch. I have graded the colors using different shades of pink, but you can use whatever colors you like or just work with one shade.

Materials

- Rico Baby Cotton Soft DK
  - 1 x 50g ball in shade 53 Flamingo (yarn A)
  - 1 x 50g ball in shade 21 Fuchsia (yarn B)
  - 1 x 50g ball in shade 30 Candy Pink (yarn C)
- Knitting needles size 3.25mm (US 3, UK 10)
- Large-eyed sewing needle
- 1 button

. . . .

Gauge: 22 sts x 42 rows measures 4 in. (10cm) using 3.25mm (US 3, UK 10) needles

Measurements: To fit ages 0– 6 months. Total length is 11 in. (28cm)

Abbreviations: See page 27

Special Abbreviation: k2togtbl = knit 2 stitches together through the back loops

START AT THE BOTTOM POINT OF BIB

Using 3.25mm (US 3, UK 10) needles
and yarn A, cast on 3 sts. Knit.
Next Row: K1, kfb, k1.
Next Row: Knit.
Next Row: Sl1, k1, yfwd, k to end.
Rep last row to 46 sts.
Change to yarn B.
Next Row: Sl1, k1, yfwd, k2tog, k to
last 4 sts, k2togtbl, yfwd, k2.
Next Row: Sl1, k to end.
Rep last 2 rows for 32 rows.
Change to yarn C.
Continue to work 6 more rows
as before.

Next Row: Sl1, k1, yfwd, sl1, k2tog, psso. K to last 5 sts, sl1, k2tog, psso, yfwd, k2.

Next Row: Knit.

Rep last 2 rows to 36 sts.

Next Row: Sl1, k1, yfwd, k2tog, k7, bind off next 14 sts, k7, k2tog, yfwd, k2,

Work on last set of 11 sts for first strap.

Next Row: K7, k2tog, k2 (10 sts).

Next Row: K2, k2tog, k6 (9 sts).

Next Row: K5, k2tog, k2 (8 sts).

Next Row: K2, k2tog, k2tog, yfwd, k2 (7 sts).

Next Row: Knit.

Next Row: K3, k2tog, yfwd, k2.

Next Row: Knit.

Rep last 2 rows 14 more rows.

Next Row (buttonhole row): K3, yfwd, k2tog, k to end.

Next Row: Knit.

Next Row: Knit. Bind off.

Rejoin yarn to rem 11 sts for second strap. Work to match first strap but omit buttonhole row. Work ends in neatly.

Flower

Using 3.25mm (US 3, UK 10) needles and yarn C, cast on 55 sts.

Knit 2 rows.

BIND OFF AS FOLLOWS

K2, slip first st over second st, * yfwd, slip st over yfwd, k1, bind off next st in normal way. Rep from * until all stitches are bound off. Fasten off.

Piece will coil as you bind off. Coil into flower shape and secure with a few stitches. Sew flower to side of bib.

Attach button to correspond with buttonhole.

Sleepy Babies Blanket

This cute and novel blanket is made using different colored and textured squares. I have chosen cream and beige, but you can choose whatever colors suit your décor. The little sleepy babies add a fun element to the finished project. Again, it's easy an easy project: the blanket is made in strips that are joined together. The faces are made and stitched onto the main blanket afterward.

Materials

- ✂ King Cole Comfort Chunky (bulky weight), 137 yds. (125m)
  - 3 x 100g balls in shade 426 Cream (yarn A)
  - 2 x 100g balls in shade 429 Cork (yarn B)
- ✂ King Cole Cuddles Chunky Yarn (bulky weight), 137 yds. (125m)
  - 2 x 100g balls in shade 3140 Toffee (yarn C)
  - ✂ Small amounts of DK weight yarn in varying colors to make the faces
  - ✂ Knitting needles size 5.50mm (US 9, UK 5) and 4.00mm (US 6, UK 8)
  - ✂ Large-eyed sewing needle
  - ✂ Small pom-pom maker

Gauge: 25 sts x 42 rows measures 7 in. (18cm) square using 5.50mm (US 9, UK 5) needles

Measurements: 21 in. wide x 35 in. long (54 x 85cm)

Abbreviations: See page 27

Stripes

EACH STRIP IS WORKED FROM BASE TO TOP OF BLANKET

Using 5.50mm (US 9, UK 5) needles, cast on 25 sts and work strips as follows.

Strip 1: Work 5 reps of 42 rows each in sequence B, A, C, A, B.

Strip 2: Work 5 reps of 42 rows each in sequence A, C, B, A, A.

Strip 3: Work 5 reps of 42 rows each in sequence C, B, A, C, B.

TO WORK STRIPED TURNOVER

Using 5.50mm (US 9, UK 5) needles and yarn A, cast on 12 sts.

Work 4 rows in garter stitch; join in yarn B.

Work 2 rows in B and 2 rows in A until strip, when slightly stretched, fits across width of blanket, ending with 4 rows of A. Bind off.

A	A	A
B	A	C
C	B	A
A	C	B
B	A	C

Babies' Heads

LARGE WITH STRIPED HAT

Using 4.00mm (US 6, UK 8) needles and your chosen color, cast on 12 sts.

Inc 1 st at each end on next and every foll alt row to 24 sts.

Work 16 rows straight, join in contrasts, and work 4 rows blue, 2 rows white.

Rep last 6 rows once more. Continue in blue.

Dec 1 st at each end of every row to 12 sts. Bind off.

LARGE WITH HATBAND

Work as striped hat, but use just one color yarn.

BAND FOR HAT

Using 4.00mm (US 6, UK 8) needles and color to match hat, cast on 4 sts. Work in garter stitch until strip fits across width of hat. Bind off.

SMALL HEAD

Using 4.00mm (US 6, UK 8) needles and your chosen color, cast on 12 sts.

Inc as for large head to 20 sts.

Finishing

Work in all ends neatly. Join strips together to form blanket. Sew the turnover strip to the blanket, using the picture as a guide. Work in ends on faces. Sew hatband in place onto hat. Embroider sleeping eyes and a mouth on each face. Make tiny pom-poms and sew to the top of each hat. Place the heads in the center of the top three squares of the blanket. Sew in place.

Work 14 rows in garter stitch.
Change to contrast color.
Work 8 rows in garter stitch.
Dec 1 st at each end of every row to
    12 sts. Bind off.

Pinafore Dress

Cream and pale green are teamed together to create this special little pinafore dress. The skirt is shaped neatly and little shoulders straps complete the project. Add a tiny heart-shaped pocket for decoration. It is all worked in garter stitch, with the added interest of a slipped stitch pattern at the hemline.

Materials

- King Cole Comfort DK (light worsted weight)
  - 1 x 100g ball in shade 1732 Basil (yarn A)
  - 1 x 100g ball in shade 585 Cream (yarn B)
- Knitting needles size 3.75mm (US 4, UK 9)
- Large-eyed sewing needle
- 2 buttons

Gauge: 21 sts x 42 rows measures 4 in. (10cm) using 3.75mm (US 4, UK 9) needles

Measurements: To fit chest size 16 in.–18 in. (41–46cm) and length 14 in. (36cm)

Abbreviations: See page 27

Special Abbreviations: yb = yarn to back of work; yf = yarn to front of work

NOTE: When slipping stitches, remember to bring the yarn either to the back or front of the work as stated.

Heart Pocket

Using 3.75mm (US 4, UK 9) needles
and yarn A, cast on 2 sts.
Next Row: Knit.
Next Row: Kfb twice.
Next Row: Knit.
Next Row: Kfb, k2, kfb.
Next Row: Knit.
Next Row: Kfb, knit to last st, kfb.
Next Row: Knit.
Continue as on last 2 rows until you
have 18 sts.
Work 8 rows in garter stitch.

FIRST HALF OF HEART

Next Row: K2tog, k5, k2tog; turn,
leaving rem 9 sts for second half of
heart.
Next Row: K7.
Next Row: K2tog, k3, k2tog.
Next Row: K2tog, k1, k2tog.
Next Row: Sl1, k2tog, psso. Fasten off.
Rejoin A to rem 9 sts and complete
second half of heart to match first
half.

Finishing

Work in ends. Sew side seams
on dress. Sew on buttons on to
correspond with buttonholes. Attach
pocket to front of dress.

Sailboat Bib

This pretty bib will need a little more concentration when increasing and decreasing, but the main part of the project is still using garter stitch. I have added a simple appliqué of a sailing boat that is knitted and sewn onto the bib when completed.

Materials

- Rico Baby Cotton Soft DK (worsted weight), 137 yds. (125m)
  - 1 x 50g ball in shade 37 Navy Blue (yarn A)
  - 1 x 50g ball in shade 03 Light Blue (yarn B)
- Small amounts of Rico Baby Cotton Soft DK in shades 01 White, 35 Red, and 23 Jeans
- Knitting needles size 3.25mm (US 3, UK 10)
- Large-eyed sewing needle
- 1 button

Gauge: 22 sts x 42 rows measures 4 in. (10cm) using 3.25mm (US 3, UK 10) needles

Measurements: To fit age 0–6 months; length 11 in. (28cm)

Abbreviations: See page 27

Special Abbreviation: k2togtbl = knit 2 stitches together through the back loops

Bib

START AT BOTTOM POINT OF BIB

Using 3.25mm (US 3, UK 10) needles and yarn A, cast on 3 sts. Knit.

Next Row: K1, kfb, k1.

Next Row: Knit.

Next Row: Sl1, k1, yfwd, k to end.

Rep last row to 46 sts.

Change to yarn B.

Next Row: Sl1, k1, yfwd, k2tog, k to last 4 sts, k2togtbl, yfwd, k2.

Next Row: Sl1, k to end.

Rep last 2 rows for 38 rows.

Next Row: Sl1, k1, yfwd, sl1, k2tog, psso, k to last 5 sts, sl1, k2tog, psso, yfwd, k2.

Next Row: Knit.

Rep last 2 rows to 36 sts.

Next Row: Sl1, k1, yfwd, k2tog, k7, bind off next 14 sts, k7, k2tog, yfwd, k2.

Work on last set of 11 sts for first strap.

Next Row: K7, k2tog, k2 (10 sts).

Next Row: K2, k2tog, k6 (9 sts).

Next Row: K5, k2tog, k2 (8 sts).

Next Row: K2, k2tog, k2tog, yfwd, k2 (7 sts).

Next Row: Knit.

Next Row: K3, k2tog, yfwd, k2.

Next Row: Knit.

Rep last 2 rows for 14 rows more.

Next Row (buttonhole row): K3, yfwd, k2tog, k to end.

Next Row: Knit.

Next Row: Knit. Bind off.

Rejoin yarn to rem 11 sts. Work to match first strap, but omit buttonhole row. Work ends in neatly.

Boat

LARGE SAIL

Using 3.25mm (US 3, UK 10) needles and white yarn, cast on 2 sts.

Next Row: Knit.

Next Row: Kfb, k1 (3 sts).

Next Row: Knit.

Next Row: Kfb, k to last st, kfb (5 sts).

Next Row: Knit.

Continue to inc as on last 2 rows until you have 21 sts.

Knit 1 row and bind off.

SMALL SAIL

Work as large sail, but inc to 15 sts.
  Bind off.

BOAT

Using 3.25mm (US 3, UK 10) needles
  and jeans-colored yarn, cast on 12
  sts.
Knit 2 rows.
Next Row: Kfb, k to last st, kfb.
Next Row: Knit.
Rep last row to 20 sts.
Knit 4 rows and bind off.

FLAG

Using 3.25mm (US 3, UK 10) needles
  and red yarn, cast on 8 sts.
Knit 1 row.
Next Row: K2tog, k to end.
Next Row: K to last 2 sts, k2tog.
Next Row: K2tog, k to end.
Bind off.

Finishing

Work in all ends. Sew boat appliqué
onto front of bib, using the photo as
a guide. Attach button to correspond
with buttonhole.

Christmas Shoes

These dear little shoes take just one evening to make and look so
cute with their added tiny bows. Most novice knitters will
be able to attempt them with a little concentration.

Materials

- 1 x 50g ball Sirdar Snuggly DK (worsted weight) in
  shade 242 Flamenco, 180 yds. (165m) (yarn A)
- 1 x 50g ball Sirdar Snuggly Snowflake DK
  (worsted weight) in shade 630 Milky (yarn B)
- Knitting needles size 3.25mm (US 3, UK 10)
- Large-eyed sewing needle
- 2 buttons

Gauge: 22 sts x 40 rows measures 4 in. (10cm)
using 3.25mm (US 3, UK 10) needles

Measurements: To fit ages 0–3 months.
Sole measures approx. 3 in. (8cm)

Abbreviations: See page 27

Special Abbreviation: m1 = pick up the horizontal strand of
yarn between the stitch just knitted and the next stitch on the
needle, and knit into the back of it, thus increasing one stitch

Left Shoe

Using 3.25mm (US 3, UK 10) needles and yarn A, cast on 33 sts.

Next Row: Knit.

Next Row: K1, m1, k15, m1, k1, m1, k15, m1, k1 (37 sts).

Next Row: Knit.

Next Row: K2, m1, k15, m1, k3, m1, k15, m1, k2 (41 sts).

Next Row: Knit.

Next Row: K3, m1, k15, m1, k5, m1, k15, m1, k3 (45 sts).

Next Row: Knit.

Next Row: K4, m1, k15, m1, k7, m1, k15, m1, k4 (49 sts).

Using yarn B, work 2 rows.

Change to A and work 16 rows in garter stitch.

Next Row: K16, (skp) 4 times, k1, (k2tog) 4 times, k16 (41 sts).

Next Row: Knit.

Next Row: K10, bind off 21 sts, k across rem 10 sts. (This includes 1 st after binding off.) ***

Slip first set of 10 sts on holder.

Knit 3 rows in garter stitch on rem sts and bind off.

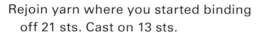

Rejoin yarn where you started binding off 21 sts. Cast on 13 sts.

Next Row: Knit across cast on sts and 10 sts from holder (23 sts).

Next Row (buttonhole row): K18, k2tog, yfwd, k3.

Next Row: Knit.

Bind off.

Right Shoe

Work same as for left shoe to ***. Leave first set of 10 sts on holder.

Next Row: K10 sts on needle; turn work and cast on 13 sts at end of row.

Next Row: K23 sts.

Next Row (buttonhole row): K18, yfwd, k2tog, k3.

Next Row: K23 sts.

Bind off all sts on needle. Rejoin yarn to sts on holder.

Knit 3 rows. Bind off.

Bows (make 2 alike)

Using 3.25mm (US 3, UK 10) needles, cast on 8 sts.

Work 32 rows in garter stitch and bind off.

Finishing

Sew seams on shoes. Sew on buttons to match buttonholes. Take a bow and run a gathering thread through the center of the piece, pulling up tight to form bow. Secure. Add a tiny white French knot in the middle of each bow. Sew to front of shoes.

Ducky Snuggle Blankie

This project looks quite complicated, but it is simply made from squares and triangles that are sewn together to form an octagon shape. The cute duckling's head is made and sewn on afterward. The squares are formed by shaping in the center of the work.

Materials

- ⚑ 1 x 100g ball King Cole Comfort DK (worsted weight) in shade 1732 Basil, 340 yds. (310m) (yarn A)
- ⚑ 1 x 50g ball King Cole Comfort DK yarn in shade 581 Lemon (yarn B)
- ⚑ Small amount of DK yarn in shades 144 Orange and 048 Black DK (for features)
- ⚑ Small amount of child-safe stuffing for duck's head
- ⚑ Knitting needles size 4.00mm (US 6, UK 8)
- ⚑ Large-eyed sewing needle

....

Gauge: Not critical on this project
Measurements: Square measures 4 in. (10cm)
Abbreviations: See page 27

Blanket (make first)

This is made up of 5 squares and 4 triangles that are sewn together.

SQUARES (MAKE 5)

Using 4.00mm (US 6, UK 8) needles and yarn A, cast on 39 sts.

Row 1: Knit.

Row 2: K18, sl1, k2tog, psso, k18.

Row 3: Knit.

Row 4: K17, sl1, k2tog, psso, k17.

Row 5: Knit.

Row 6: K16, sl1, k2tog, psso, k16.

Continue as set, working 1 less st on each side of the center dec until row [k1, sl1, k2tog, psso, k1] with 3 sts rem.

Next Row: Knit.

Next Row: Sl1, k2tog, psso. Fasten off.

Make 4 more squares in the same way.

TRIANGLES (MAKE 4)

Using 4.00mm (US 6, UK 8) needles and A, cast on 3 sts.

Row 1: Knit.

Row 2: K1, kfb, k1 (4 sts).

Row 3: Knit.

Row 4: Sl1, kfb, k to end.

Rep last row until you have 30 sts. Bind off.

Make 3 more triangles in the same way.

Duck

HEAD

Using 4.00mm (US 6, UK 8) needles and B, cast on 8 sts.

Next Row: Knit.

Next Row: Kfb in each st to end (16 sts).

Next Row: Knit.

Next Row: * K1, kfb, rep from * to end (24 sts).

Next Row: Knit.

Next Row: * K2, kfb, rep from * to end (32 sts).

Next Row: Knit.

Next Row: * K3, kfb, rep from * to end (40 sts).

Work 17 rows in garter stitch.

Next Row: * K3, k2tog, rep from * to end (32 sts).

Next Row: Knit.

Next Row: * K2, k2tog, rep from * to end (24 sts).

Next Row: Knit.

Next Row: *K1, k2tog, rep from * to end (16 sts).

Next Row: Knit.

Next Row: K2tog across row (8 sts).

Next Row: Knit.

Break yarn and draw through sts on needles. Pull up tight and fasten off.

BEAK

Using 4.00mm (US 6, UK 8) needles and orange yarn, cast on 12 sts.

Next Row: Knit.

Next Row: Kfb, knit to last st, kfb.

Rep last row to 18 sts.

Next Row: Knit.

Now k2tog at each end of every row until there are 8 sts.

Next Row: Knit. Bind off.

Finishing

Assemble blanket first. Place 3 squares in a vertical line, one on top of the other. Sew the pieces together. Now sew a square on either side of the center square in the line. This forms a cross shape. Sew a triangle into each of the four spaces left. This forms an octagon shape.

Make duck's head. Sew seam that runs down the back of the head. Stuff and form into a nice, round shape before closing. Take the beak section and fold in half lengthways. Form into a curve and pin in place on the front of the duck's head. Sew in place. Using black thread, embroider eyes on either side of the beak. Sew the head to the center square of the blanket very firmly.

Toasty Mittens on a Rope

Every little one needs some mittens to keep tiny hands toasty warm on cold days. They are quite easy to make and have the added extra of a "rope" that, when threaded through the child's coat sleeves, will prevent the mittens from getting lost when out on walks.

Materials

- ✂ 1 x 100g ball of King Cole Comfort Baby DK (worsted weight) either in shade 1964 Coral or 3108 Golden, 340 yds. (310m)
- ✂ Small amount of brown DK yarn (for smiley face; optional)
- ✂ Knitting needles size 3.75mm (US 4, UK 9)
- ✂ Large-eyed sewing needle

....

Gauge: 22 sts x 40 rows measures 4 in. (10cm) using 3.75mm (US 4, UK 9) needles

Measurements: To fit ages 6–12 months

Abbreviations: See page 27

Special Abbreviations: m1 = pick up the horizontal strand of yarn between the stitch just knitted and the next stitch on the needle, and knit into the back of it, thus increasing one stitch; k2togtbl = knit 2 stitches together through the back loops

Instructions

Using 3.75mm (US 4, UK 9) needles, cast on 30 sts.

Knit 14 rows in garter stitch. **

Right Mitten

SHAPE THUMB

Next Row: K16, m1, k1, m1, k13.
Next and foll alt rows: Knit.
Next Row: K16, m1, k3, m1, k13.
Next Row: K16, m1, k5, m1, k13.
Next Row: K16, m1, k7, m1, k13.
Next Row: K38.

WORK THUMB

Next Row: K25, turn, cast on 1 st.
Next Row: K10, turn, cast on 1 st.
Work 5 more rows on these sts.

Next Row: (K2tog) 5 times, k1.
Next Row: (K2tog) 3 times, break thread and run through sts. Fasten off.
Sew thumb seam.
*** With right side facing, rejoin yarn, pick up 2 sts from base of thumb, and knit across sts on left-hand needle (30 sts).
Work 11 rows in garter stitch.
Next Row: K1, k2tog, k10, k2tog, k2togtbl, k10, k2tog, k1.
Next Row: Knit.
Next Row: K1, k2tog, k8, k2tog, k2togtbl, k8, k2tog, k1.
Next Row: Knit.
Next Row: K1, k2tog, k6, k2tog, k2togtbl, k6, k2tog, k1.
Next Row: Knit.

Next Row: K1, k2tog, k4, k2tog, k2togtbl, k4, k2tog, k1.
Next Row: Knit. Bind off.

Left Mitten

Work as right mitten to **.

SHAPE THUMB

Row 1: K13, m1, k1, m1, k16.
Next and following alt rows: Knit.
Next Row: K13, m1, k3, m1, k16.
Next Row: K13, m1, k5, m1, k16.
Next Row: K13, m1, k7, m1, k16.
Next Row: Knit.

WORK THUMB

Next Row: K22, turn, cast on 1 st.
Next Row: K10, cast on 1 st.
Work 5 more rows on these sts.

Next Row: (K2tog) 5 times, k1.
Next Row: (K2tog) 3 times, break thread and run through sts. Fasten off.
Sew thumb seam.
Now complete as right mitten from ***.

Finishing

Sew side seam of each mitten. Embroider a smiley face on the back of mittens if you like, or just leave them plain. Make a twisted rope using lengths of yarn (see page 25). The rope needs to fit through the sleeves of the child's coat and have enough length for movement when the mittens are being worn. Attach the rope to each mitten very securely.

Navy Striped Bib

Although this bib is worked all in garter stitch, it has an added pattern using a slipped stitch that carries the colors from one shade to the next. It's very simple but gives an attractive finish to the stripes.

Materials

- ✗ Rico Baby Cotton Soft DK (worsted weight)
  - 1 x 50g ball in shade 35 Red (yarn A)
  - 1 x 50g ball in shade 19 Yellow (yarn B)
  - 1 x 50g ball in shade 37 Navy Blue (yarn C)
- ✗ Knitting needles size 3.25mm (US 3, UK 10)
- ✗ 1 button

....

Gauge: 20 sts x 40 rows measures 4 in. (10cm) using 3.25mm (US 3, UK 10) needles

Measurements: Length 9 in. (23cm) from base

Abbreviations: See page 27

Special Abbreviations: yf = bring yarn to front of work; yb = bring yarn to back of work; k2togtbl = knit 2 stitches together through the back loops

Instructions

Using 3.25mm (US 3, UK 10) needles and yarn C, cast on 43 sts.

Knit 7 rows.

Change to yarn B.

**Row 1: * K3, sl1, rep from * to last 3 sts, k3.

Row 2: * K3, yb, sl1, yf, rep from * to last 3 sts, k3.

Knit 6 rows. **

Change to yarn A.

Work from ** to **.

Change to C and work from ** to **.

Work a further 24 rows in garter stitch in C.

Using A, work from ** to **.

Using B, work Rows 1 and 2.

Knit 2 rows.

Next Row: Sl1, k1, yfwd, k2tog, k to last 4 sts, k2togtbl, yfwd, k2.

Next Row: Sl1, k to end.

Rep last 2 rows for 38 rows.

Next Row: Sl1, k1, yfwd, sl1, k2tog, psso, k to last 5 sts, sl1, k2tog, psso, yfwd, k2.

Next Row: Knit.

Rep last 2 rows to 35 sts.

Next Row: Sl1, k1, yfwd, k2tog, k7, bind off next 13 sts, k7, k2tog, yfwd, k2.

Work on last set of sts for first strap.
Next Row: K7, k2tog, k2.
Next Row: K2, k2tog, k6.
Next Row: K5, k2tog, k2.
Next Row: K2, k2tog, k2tog, yfwd, k2 (7 sts).
Next Row: Knit.
Next Row: K3, k2tog, yfwd, k2.
Next Row: Knit.
Rep last 2 rows for 14 more rows.
Next Row (buttonhole row): K3, yfwd, k2tog, k to end.

Next Row: Knit.
Next Row: Knit. Bind off.
Rejoin yarn to rem 11 sts. Work to match first strap, but omit buttonhole row. Work ends in neatly.

Finishing
Sew in all loose ends neatly. Attach button to correspond with buttonhole.

Sleepy Cow Hat and Drawstring Mittens

This sweet little hat and mittens set will make a lovely gift for a new baby. Made in the softest wool yarn, it will keep an infant warm and cozy on outings. Using a contrasting color to cast on makes a neat edging to add interest. The cute, sleepy cow appliqué makes the set even more appealing. You can, of course, just make the set plain if you prefer.

Materials

⚒ Rico Baby Classic DK (worsted weight)
- 2 x 50g balls in shade 01 White (yarn A)
- 1 x 50g ball in shade 43 Silver Gray (yarn B)
- Small amounts in shades 04 Rose, 99 Black, and 053 Beige for cow's face
⚒ Small amount of child-safe stuffing to pad face of cow
⚒ Knitting needles size 3.25mm (US 3, UK 10)
⚒ Large-eyed sewing needle

Gauge: 22 sts x 42 rows measures 4 in. (10cm) using 3.25mm (US 3, UK 10) needles

Measurements: To fit ages 0–3 months. Hat circumference approx. 14 in. (35cm)

Abbreviations: See page 27

Special Abbreviation: k2togtbl = knit 2 stitches together through the back loops

Hat

Using 3.25mm (US 3, UK 10) needles
and yarn B, cast on 72 sts.
Change to yarn A.
Continue in garter stitch until work
measures 6½ in. (17cm).

SHAPE CROWN AS FOLLOWS

Row 1: * K10, skp, rep from * to end.
**Row 2 and alt (even-numbered) foll
rows:** Knit.
Row 3: * K9, skp, rep from * to end.
Row 5: * K8, skp, rep from * to end.
Row 7: * K7, skp, rep from * to end.
Row 9: * K6, skp, rep from * to end.
Row 11: * K5, skp, rep from * to end.
Row 13: * K4, skp, rep from * to end.

Row 15: * K3, skp, rep from * to end.
Row 17: * K2, skp, rep from * to end.
Row 19: * K1, skp, rep from * to end.
Row 20: K2tog across row. Break
yarn and run through rem 6 sts on
needle, draw up, and fasten off.

Mittens (make 2 alike)

Using 3.25mm (US 3, UK 10) needles
and yarn B, cast on 32 sts.
Change to yarn A.
Work 38 rows in garter stitch.

SHAPE TOP

Next Row: K1, k2tog, k11, k2tog,
k2togtbl, k11, k2tog, k1.
Next Row: Knit.

Next Row: K1, k2tog, k9, k2tog, k2togtbl, k9, k2tog, k1.
Next Row: Knit.
Next Row: K1, k2tog, k7, k2tog, k2togtbl, k7, k2tog, k1.
Next Row: Knit. Bind off.

Cow's Head Appliqué

HEAD

Using 3.25mm (US 3, UK 10) needles and A, cast on 8 sts.
Next Row: Knit.
Next Row: Kfb, k to last st, kfb.
Rep last row until you have 20 sts.
Work 24 rows in garter stitch.
Next Row: K2tog at each end of row.

Rep last row until 8 sts rem. Bind off.

NOSE

Using 3.25mm (US 3, UK 10) needles and pink yarn, cast on 6 sts.

Knit 1 row.

Next Row: Kfb, k to last st, kfb.

Rep last row to 14 sts.

Work 14 rows in garter stitch on these sts.

Next Row: K2tog, k to last 2 sts, k2tog.

Rep last row to 8 sts.

Next Row: Knit. Bind off.

EARS (MAKE 2 ALIKE)

Using 3.25mm (US 3, UK 10) needles and black yarn, cast on 3 sts.

Next Row: Knit.

Next Row: Kfb, k1, kfb.

Next Row: Knit.

Next Row: Kfb, k3, kfb (7 sts).
Knit 2 rows.
Next row: K2tog, k3, k2tog.
Next Row: Knit.
Next Row: K2tog, k1, k2tog.
Next Row: Sl1, k2tog, psso, fasten off.

HORNS

Using 3.25mm (US 3, UK 10) needles
and brown yarn, cast on 3 sts.
Next Row: Knit.
Next Row: Kfb, k1, kfb.
Next Row: Knit.
Next Row: Kfb, k3, kfb (7 sts).
Next Row: Knit.
Knit 14 more rows in garter stitch.
Next Row: K2tog, k3, k2tog.
Next Row: Knit.
Next Row: K2tog, k1, k2tog.
Next Row: Knit.
Next Row: Sl1, k2tog, psso. Fasten off.

CENTER HEAD SECTION

Using 3.25mm (US 3, UK 10) needles
and yarn A, cast on 7 sts.
Knit 25 rows and bind off.

Finishing

HAT

Sew seam on hat that will run down
the center back, reversing last 2 in.
(5cm) for turned-back brim.

MITTENS

Sew side seam on mittens. Make a
twisted cord with yarn B (see page
25), and thread through fabric at wrist
level. Tie in a bow.

COW APPLIQUÉ

Work in ends on pieces. Take head
and place pink nose sideways on
lower part. Add a small piece of
stuffing to pad out nose very lightly.
Sew in place. Take horns and roll them
into a cylinder shape. Wrap the center
section around the horns and secure
it with a few stitches. Curl horns
outward at each side. Sew to top of
head. Pleat ears at base. Sew an ear
to each side of head. Embroider eyes
and nostrils using black yarn. Sew
head to front of hat.

Striped Yoke Cardigan

Neat stripes and contrast edging make this little cardigan a bit more of a challenge. You will need to use separate balls of yarns for color changes, so this project is aimed more at the experienced knitter. For those of you who don't feel confident enough to work the contrasting stripes, you can always make the cardigan using one shade.

Materials

- Sirdar Snuggly DK (light worsted weight), 179 yds. (165m)
  - 2 [2, 3] x 50g balls in shade 251 White (yarn A)
  - 1 [1, 1] x 50g ball in shade 482 Bubbles Blue (yarn B)
- Knitting needles size 3.75mm (US 4, UK 9)
- Large-eyed sewing needle
- 3 buttons
- Stitch holders

....

Gauge: 20 sts x 40 rows measures 4 in. (10cm) using 3.75mm (US 4, UK 9) needles

Measurements: To fit chest size 16 [18, 20] in. (41 [46, 51] cm); length 8 [9, 10] in. (20 [23, 26] cm); sleeve seam 4½ [5, 5½] in. (12 [13, 14] cm).

Abbreviations: See page 27

NOTE: Side and sleeve seams are adjustable.

Back

Using 3.75mm (US 4, UK 9) needles
  and yarn B, cast on 42 [48, 54] sts.
Work 7 rows in garter stitch (Row 1 is
  RS of work).
Change to yarn A and continue in
  garter stitch until work measures
  5 [5½, 6] in. (12.5 [14, 15] cm) or
  desired length, ending on a WS row.
  Mark each end of this row as start of
  armhole shaping.

SHAPE RAGLAN ARMHOLES

Join in B and work in stripes of 2 rows
  B, 2 rows A.
Row 1: K2, sl1, psso, k to last 4 sts,
  k2tog, k2.

Row 2: Knit.

Rep last 2 rows until you have 14 [16, 18] sts.

Leave sts on holder for back neck.

Left Front

Using 3.75mm (US 4, UK 9) needles and B, cast on 23 [26, 29] sts.

Work 7 rows in garter stitch.

You will now work the main piece in A, and using a small ball of B, work the contrast front band.

When changing colors, make sure you twist the yarns together on the wrong side of the work to avoid holes in the fabric.

Next Row: Using A, k to last 4 sts, k4 B.

Next Row: K4 B, change to A, k to end.

Continue as set until front measures the same as back to marker.

Beg with yarn B, you will now work in stripes of yarns A and B as on the back and at the same time keeping the 4 border stitches in yarn B.

SHAPE RAGLAN ARMHOLE

Next Row: K2, sl1, k1, psso, k to last 4 sts, k4 B.

Next Row: K4 B, k to end.

Continue as on last 2 rows until you have 13 [14, 15] sts, ending at the front edge.

SHAPE NECK

Work 4 [5, 6] sts and slip these onto a holder for neckband. Work to end.

Continue to dec at raglan as before and at the same time, dec 1 st at neck edge on next 3 rows.

Work 1 more raglan shaping dec.

K3tog and fasten off.

Mark positions for 2 buttons on the left front. The first should come 2¾ in. (7cm) below neck shaping, allowing for the third buttonhole to be worked ¼ in. (0.5cm) above sts on holder. Space second button halfway between.

Right Front

Using 3.75mm (US 4, UK 9) needles
and B, cast on 23 [26, 29] sts.
Work 7 rows in garter stitch.
You will now work the main piece in
A, and, using a small ball of B, work
the contrast front band.
When changing colors, make sure
you twist the yarns together on the
wrong side of the work to avoid
holes in the fabric.
Next Row: K4 B, using A k to end.
Next Row: Using A, k to last 4 sts,
k4 B.

Continue as set until front measures
the same as back to marker.
Now complete to match left front,
reversing shaping and working
buttonholes on right side rows to
match markers as follows: k2, yfwd,
k2tog.

Sleeves (make 2 alike)

Using 3.75mm (US 4, UK 9) needles
and yarn B, cast on 24 [26, 28] sts.
Work 7 rows in garter stitch. Break
yarn B and join in yarn A.
Work 4 rows in garter stitch.

Now inc 1 st at each end of next and the foll 8th [6th, 6th] row until you have 32 [36, 40] sts ending on a WS row.

Continue without further shaping until work measures 4½ [5, 5½] in. (11.5 [12.5, 14] cm) or desired length.

SHAPE RAGLAN ARMHOLES

Work raglan shaping as on back, foll same stripe sequence, until you have 4 sts left. Leave on holder for neckband.

Join raglan seams, matching stripes.

Neckband

Using 3.75mm (US 4, UK 9) needles and B, with right side facing, slip sts from right front holder onto the right-hand needle.

Join in B, pick up, and k8 sts from right front neck.

K across sts from sleeve, back neck, and sleeve, then pick up and k8 sts down left front and finally sts from holder.

Work 6 rows in garter stitch, working a buttonhole as before on Row 4. Bind off.

Finishing

Sew side and sleeve seams and sew on buttons to correspond with buttonholes.

Newborn Diaper Cover, Hat, and Booties

Create this special set for a new baby. I have used a mixture of cream and dusky pink, making this a perfect traditional look for a little girl, but it is also very easy to change the colors and omit the hearts and embroidery to give the set a totally different look.

Materials

- ✗ King Cole Comfort Baby DK (worsted weight)
  - 1 x 100g ball in shade 585 Cream (yarn A)
  - 1 x 100g ball in shade 1730 Porcelain (yarn B)
- Small amount of 1732 Basil for embroidery and pom-pom (yarn C)
- ✗ Knitting needles size 3.25mm (US 3, UK 10) and 3.75mm (US 4, UK 9)
- ✗ Large-eyed sewing needle ✗ 6 medium buttons
- ✗ 2 small buttons ✗ Small pom-pom maker

. . . .

Gauge: 22 sts x 40 rows measures 4 in. (10cm)
using 3.75mm (US 4, UK 9) needles

Measurements: To fit ages 0–3 months. The diaper cover is
16 in. width x 14 in. (41 x 36cm) completed length. The hat has a
circumference of 14 in. (36cm). The shoe sole is 3 in. (8cm) long.

Abbreviations: See page 27

Special Abbreviation: m1 = pick up the horizontal strand of
yarn between the stitch just knitted and the next stitch on the
needle, and knit into the back of it, thus increasing one stitch

Hat

Using 3.75mm (US 4, UK 9) needles and yarn B, cast on 66 sts. Break yarn B and join in yarn A.

Work in garter stitch for 56 rows. Bind off.

Diaper Cover

Using 3.75mm (US 4, UK 9) needles and B, cast on 52 sts.

Knit 5 rows.

**Next Row: K3, k2tog, yfwd, knit to last 5 sts, k2tog, yfwd, k3.

Knit 15 rows. **

Rep from ** to ** once more.

Next Row: K3, k2tog, yfwd, k to 5 sts, k2tog, yfwd, k3.

Knit 6 rows.

Bind off 6 sts at the beg of the next 2 rows (40 sts).

Next Row: K3, k2tog, k to last 5 sts, k2tog, k3.

Rep last row 5 more times (28 sts).

Next Row: K3, k2tog, k to last 5 sts, k2tog, k3.

Next Row: Knit.

Rep last 2 rows 4 more times (18 sts).

Knit 14 rows.

Next Row: K3, kfb in next st, k to last
   4 sts, kfb in next st, k3.
Next Row: Knit.
Rep last 2 rows 4 more times (28 sts).
Next Row: K3, kfb in next st, k to last
   4 sts, kfb in next st, k3.
Rep last row 5 more times (40 sts).
Continue in garter stitch until work
   measures the same as the back of
   cover. Bind off.

Shoes

LEFT SHOE

Using size 3.25mm (US 3, UK 10)
   needles and A, cast on 33 sts.
Next Row: Knit.
Next Row: K1, m1, k15, m1, k1, m1, k15,
   m1, k1 (37 sts).
Next Row: Knit.
Next Row: K2, m1, k15, m1, k3, m1,
   k15, m1, k2 (41 sts).
Next Row: Knit.
Next Row: K3, m1, k15, m1, k5, m1,
   k15, m1, k3 (45 sts).
Next Row: Knit.
Next Row: K4, m1, k15, m1, k7, m1,
   k15, m1, k4 (49 sts).
Using B, work 2 rows.
Change to A and work 14 rows in
   garter stitch.
Change to B.
Next Row: K16, (skp) 4 times, k1,
   (k2tog) 4 times, k16 (41 sts).
Next Row: Knit.

Next Row: K10, bind off 21 sts, k
   across rem 10 sts. (This includes 1 st
   after binding off.) ***
Slip first set of 10 sts on holder.
K3 rows in garter stitch on rem sts
   and bind off.
Rejoin yarn where you started binding
   off 21 sts. Cast on 13 sts.
Next Row: Knit across cast on sts and
   10 sts from holder (23 sts).
Next Row (buttonhole row): K18,
   k2tog, yfwd, k3.
Next Row: Knit.
Bind off.

RIGHT SHOE

Work same as for left shoe to ***.
   Leave first set of 10 sts on holder.

Next Row: K10 sts on needle; turn work and cast on 13 sts at end of row.

Next Row: K23 sts.

Next Row (buttonhole row): K18, yfwd, k2tog, k3.

Next Row: K23 sts.

Bind off all sts on needle. Rejoin yarn to sts on holder.

K3 rows. Bind off.

Hearts

SMALL

Using 3.25mm (US 3, UK 10) needles and B, cast on 2 sts.

Next Row: Knit.

Next Row: Kfb twice.

Next Row: Knit.

Next Row: Kfb, k2, kfb.

Next Row: Knit.

Next Row: Kfb, k to last st, kfb.

Next Row: Knit.

Continue as on last 2 rows until you have 14 sts.

Work 6 rows in garter stitch.

Next Row: K2tog, k3, k2tog, turn while leaving rem sts on holder.

Next Row: Knit.

Next Row: K2tog, k1, k2tog.

Next Row: Sl1, k2tog, psso, fasten off.

Join yarn to rem 7 sts and complete to match first side.

LARGE

Using 3.25mm (US 3, UK 10) and A, cast on 2 sts.

Next Row: Knit.

Next Row: Kfb twice.

Next Row: Knit.

Next Row: Kfb, k2, kfb.

Next Row: Knit.

Next Row: Kfb, k to last st, kfb.

Next Row: Knit.

Continue as on last 2 rows until you have 18 sts.

Work 8 rows in garter stitch.

Next Row: K2tog, k5, k2tog, turn while leaving rem sts on holder.

Next Row: Knit.

Next Row: K2tog, k3, k2tog.

Next Row: K2tog, k1, k2tog.

Next Row: Sl1, k2tog, psso. Fasten off.

Rejoin yarn to rem 7 sts and complete to match first side.

Finishing

DIAPER COVER

Take cream heart and sew in place on center front of cover. Using contrasting yarns, embroider flowers and leaves onto the heart.

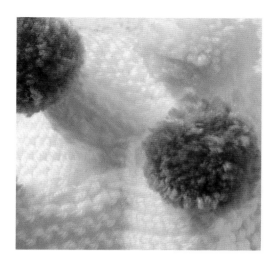

Work in ends and sew on buttons to correspond with buttonholes.

HAT

Sew center back seam. Fold hat in half with seam running up center back. Pleat each outer corner to center of hat to give four points. Make small contrasting pom-poms and sew firmly to each corner point. Sew small heart onto center front of hat.

SHOES

Work in ends. Sew seam on each shoe. Sew on buttons to correspond with buttonholes.

Teddy Bear Romper

Knit a cute romper suit just right for summer days. Team it with a cool cotton shirt and baby will be ready for an outing! Worked all in garter stitch, this project is quite easy to make. I have added a cute teddy face that is sewn on to the finished romper, but you can leave the project plain or even sew on a ready-made motif if you prefer.

Materials

- Rico Baby Classic DK (light worsted weight)
  - 2 [3] x 50g balls in shade 09 Red (yarn A)
  - Small amounts in shade 053 Beige (yarn B)
- Small amount of brown DK yarn (yarn C)
- Knitting needles size 4.00mm (US 6, UK 8)
- Large-eyed sewing needle
- 2 buttons
- Small amount of child-safe stuffing

Gauge: 20 sts x 40 rows measures 4 in. (10cm) using 4.00mm (US 6, UK 8) needles and garter stitch

Measurements: To fit ages 0–3 months [3–6 months]. The length is 15 [16½] in. (38 [42] cm); the chest is 20 [22] in. (52 [56] cm)

Abbreviations: See page 27

Special Abbreviations: m1 = pick up the horizontal strand of yarn between the stitch just knitted and the next stitch on the needle, and knit into the back of it, thus increasing one stitch; k2togtbl = knit 2 stitches together through the back loops

Front

Using 4.00mm (US 6, UK 8) needles
and yarn A, cast on 18 sts.
Work 10 rows in garter stitch.

SHAPE LEGS

Row 1 (RS): K4, m1, k to last 4 sts,
m1, k4.
Row 2 (WS): K4, m1, k to last 4 sts,
m1, k4.
Rep last 2 rows until you have 42 [50]
sts, ending on a Row 2.
Next Row: K4, m1, k to last 4 sts,
m1, k4.
Next Row: Knit.

Rep last 2 rows until you have 58 [66]
sts on the needles. ***
Continue straight in garter stitch until
piece measures 7 [8¼] in. (18 [21]
cm), ending on a WS row.

SHAPE TOP

Next Row: K8, skp, k to last 10 sts,
k2togtbl, k8.
Next Row: K8, k2togtbl, k to last 10
sts, k2togtbl, k8.
Rep last 2 rows until 32 [40] sts.
Work 12 rows in garter stitch.
Bind off.

Back

Work as Front to ***.

SHAPE BACK WITH SHORT ROWS AS FOLLOWS

Next Row: K to last 4 sts, turn.
Next Row: K to last 4 sts, turn.
Next Row: K to last 8 sts, turn.
Next Row: K to last 8 sts, turn.
Continue in this way, working 4 extra sts on subsequent rows, until you reach Row 10. K to last 20 sts. Turn.
Next Row: K across all sts.
Next Row: K across all sts.
Continue straight in garter stitch until work measures 7 [8¼] in. (18 [21] cm), ending on WS of work.

Work 12 rows in garter stitch.

WORK STRAPS

Next Row: K8, bind off 16 [24] sts, k to end.
Next Row: Work on first set of 8 sts. Leave rem 8 sts on a holder.
Work 26 [30] rows in garter stitch.
Next Row: Work buttonhole. K3, bind off 2 sts, k3.
Next Row: K3, cast on 2 sts, k3.
Work 4 rows in garter stitch. Bind off.
Rejoin yarn to sts on holder and work to match other strap.

Teddy Face

Using 3.75mm (US 4, UK 9) needles
   and B, cast on 10 sts.
Knit 1 row.
Next Row: Kfb, knit to last st, kfb.
Next Row: Knit.
Rep last 2 rows until you have 24 sts.
Work 16 rows in garter stitch.
Next Row: K2tog at each end of row.
Next Row: Knit.
Rep last 2 rows until you have 12 sts.
   Bind off.

MUZZLE

Using 3.75mm (US 4, UK 9) needles
   and B, cast on 8 sts.
Next Row: Knit.
Next Row: Kfb, k to last st, kfb.
Next Row: Knit.
Rep last 2 rows until you have 16 sts.
Work 12 rows in garter stitch.
Next Row: K2tog at each end of row.
Next Row: Knit.
Rep last 2 rows until you have 8 sts.
   Bind off.

Next Row: (K2tog) 4 times.
Bind off rem 4 sts.

NOSE

Using 3.75mm (US 4, UK 9) needles
   and B, cast on 8 sts.
Knit 4 rows.
Next Row: K2tog at each end of row
   (6 sts).
Next Row: Knit.
Rep last 2 rows until you have 4 sts.
Next Row: K2tog twice.
Next Row: K2tog. Fasten off but leave
   a long tail of yarn.

Finishing

Sew in loose ends. Join seam
at crotch. Sew side seams. Sew
on buttons to correspond with
buttonholes.

TEDDY FACE

Take muzzle and run a thread all
around the outer edge, gather up
slightly to form a cup shape, and pin to
lower part of face. Add a small piece
of stuffing to pad lightly. Sew to face.
Take nose and pin it to the correct spot
on the muzzle; sew in place. Using a
long tail of yarn, sew a line to form
muzzle. Make sure to pull quite firmly
to do this. Curl ears into cup shape and
sew to the top of the head on either
side. Embroider eyes on either side of
nose. Sew in place to front of romper.

EARS (MAKE 2 ALIKE)

Using 3.75mm (US 4, UK 9) needles
   and yarn B, cast on 8 sts.
Next Row: Knit.
Next Row: Kfb in each st to end
   (16 sts).
Next Row: Knit.
Work 10 rows in garter stitch.
Next Row: (K2tog) 8 times (8 sts).

Under-the-Sea Hooded Jacket

Make this cute and cheerful hooded jacket with an under-the-sea theme. The main jacket is just simple garter stitch. I have used some bright colors in stripes to add extra interest. When complete, knit some little fish and seaweed to embellish the fronts. I have added two fish, but you could customize your jacket by making more fish and sewing them on to suit your own design.

Materials

- ✖ 4 [4, 5, 6, 6] x 50g balls Sirdar Snuggly Doodle DK (worsted weight) in shade 206 Sprinkles, 179 yds. (165m) (yarn A)
- ✖ Sirdar Snuggly DK (worsted weight)
  - 1 x 50g ball in shade 489 Tangerine (yarn B)
  - 1 x 50g ball in shade 488 Violet (yarn C)
  - 1 x 50g ball in shade 260 Summer Lime (yarn D)
- ✖ Few yards of black yarn for embroidery of eyes on fish
- ✖ Knitting needles size 4.00mm (US 6, UK 8) and 3.75mm (US 4, UK 9) ✖ Large-eyed sewing needle ✖ 4 buttons

. . . .

Gauge: 20 sts x 40 rows measures 4 in. (10cm) using 4.00mm (US 6, UK 8) needles

Measurements: To fit chest size 16¼ [18, 20, 22, 24] in. (41 [46, 51, 56, 61] cm); length from back neck 9½ [10¼, 11½, 12½, 13¾] in. (24 [26, 29, 32, 35] cm); sleeve seam 4¾ [6, 7, 8¼, 9½] in. (12 [15, 18, 21, 24] cm)

Abbreviations: See page 27

Back

Using 4.00mm (US 6, UK 8) needles and yarn A, cast on 46 [51, 56, 61, 66] sts.

Work in garter stitch until piece measures 9½ [10¼, 11½, 12½, 13¾] in. (24 [26, 29, 32, 35] cm).

SHAPE SHOULDERS

Bind off 15 [17, 18, 20, 22] sts at beg of next 2 rows. Slip rem sts onto a holder for the back neck.

Left Front

Using 4.00mm (US 6, UK 8) needles and A, cast on 26 [28, 31, 33, 36] sts.
Continue in garter stitch until front is 18 [20, 20, 22, 24] rows less than back to shoulder shaping.

SHAPE NECK

K19 [21, 23, 25, 28] sts. Slip rem sts onto a holder. Turn.
Next Row: K2, k2tog. Knit to end.
Next Row: K to last 4 sts, k2tog, k2.

Continue to dec 1 st at neck edge as
set on the next and foll 1 [1, 2, 2, 3]
alt rows. 15 [17, 18, 20, 22] sts rem.

Continue until front matches back to
shoulder shaping. Bind off.

Right Front

Mark positions for 4 buttons on Left
Front. The first should come 6 rows
down from neck shaping, and the
last should come 8 [16, 20, 20, 22]
rows from bottom. Space 2 other
markers evenly between these
points.

To make a buttonhole: K3, yfwd,
k2tog.

Using 4.00mm (US 6, UK 8) needles
and A, cast on 26 [28, 31, 33, 36] sts.

Continue in garter stitch until front
is 18 [20, 20, 22, 24] rows less
than back to shoulder shaping,
remembering to make buttonholes
as stated at appropriate points to
match markers.

SHAPE NECK

Next Row: K7 [7, 8, 8, 8] sts, slip onto
a holder for neck, knit to end of row.
Turn.

Next Row: K to last 4 sts, k2tog, k2.

Next Row: K2, k2tog, k to end.

Continue to dec 1 st at neck edge as
set on the next and foll 1 [1, 2, 2, 3]
alt rows. 15 [17, 18, 20, 22] sts rem.

Continue until front matches back to
shoulder shaping. Bind off.

Plain Sleeve

Using 4.00mm (US 6, UK 8) needles
and yarn A, cast on 28 [29, 30, 31,
32] sts.

Work in garter stitch for 6 [6, 8, 8, 10]
rows.

Now inc 1 st at each end of the next
and foll 6th rows until you have 40
[43, 52, 55, 64] sts.

Continue without further inc until
sleeve measures 4¾ [6, 7, 8¼, 9½] in.
(12 [15, 18, 21, 24] cm) or required
length. Bind off quite loosely.

Striped Sleeve

Using 4.00mm (US 6, UK 8) needles
and A, cast on 28 [29, 30, 31, 32] sts.
Work in garter stitch for 6 [6, 8, 8,
10] rows.
Work in striped sequence of 2 rows B,
2 rows A, 2 rows C, 2 rows A, and at
the same time inc 1 st at each end of
row on next and foll 6 rows until you
have 40 [43, 52, 55, 64] sts.
Continue without further increase
until sleeve measures 4¾ [6, 7,
8¼, 9½] in. (12 [15, 18, 21, 24]
cm) or required length. Bind off
quite loosely.

Hood

Join shoulders using a flat seam.
With right side facing and using
4.00mm (US 6, UK 8) needles and
A, slip sts from right front neck onto
right-hand needle. Rejoin yarn and
pick up and k11 [13, 15, 15, 17] sts up
right front neck. Work across back
neck, inc as follows: (k1, inc in next
st) 8 [8, 10, 10, 11] times, inc 0 [1, 0, 1,
0], pick up and k11 [13, 15, 15, 17] sts
down left front, and finally k across
sts on holder from neck.
Next Row: Knit.
Bind off 6 [6, 8, 8, 8] sts at beg of next
2 rows.

Continue in garter stitch for a further 3¼ in. (8cm).

Next Row: K4, m1, k to last 4 sts, m1, k4.

Work 5 rows in garter stitch.

Continue as on last 6 rows until you have 58 [66, 77, 78, 86] sts.

Work a further 1½ in. (4cm) in garter stitch.

SHAPE CROWN

Next Row: K27 [31, 34, 37, 41], skp, k2tog, k27 [31, 34, 37, 41].

Knit 3 rows.

Next Row: K26 [30, 33, 36, 40], skp, k2tog, k27 [31, 34, 37, 41].

Knit 3 rows.

Continue to dec in center as set on every 4th row, until you have 50 [58, 64, 70, 78] sts.

Bind off.

Sew seam on hood.

HOOD EDGING

With wrong side of Hood facing, and using 4.00mm (US 6, UK 8) needles, rejoin A to right-hand side of work at Neck Edge. Pick up and k1 st from

each row end across Hood. Work 12 [14, 14, 16, 16] rows in garter stitch using the same stripe sequence as on Sleeve. Bind off evenly. Fold brim back onto Hood and stitch in place on either side and in the center.

Fish (make 2; 1 in yarn B and 1 in yarn C)

Using 3.75mm (US 4, UK 9) needles and appropriate shade, cast on 2 sts.
Next Row: Knit.
Next Row: Kfb twice.
Next Row: Knit.
Next Row: Kfb, k2, kfb.
Next Row: Knit.
Next Row: Kfb, k4, kfb.
Knit 10 rows.
Next Row: K2tog at each end of row.
Rep last row to 4 sts.
Next Row: (Kfb) 4 times.
Next Row: Knit.
Next Row: Kfb, k6, kfb.
Next Row: Knit.
Next Row: Kfb, k8, kfb.
Knit 2 rows and bind off.

SEAWEED

Using 3.75mm (US 4, UK 9) needles and yarn D, cast on 3 sts.
Knit 4 rows.
**Next Row: Bind off 2 sts.
Next Row: Cast on 2 sts.
Knit 4 rows. ******

Rep from ** to ** for desired length, then bind off.

Finishing

Fold sleeves in half and mark center point. Pin center of sleeve to center of shoulder seam. Sew sleeves to back and fronts, making sure they are even on either side. Sew side and sleeve seams. Turn back brim of hood and secure with a few stitches. Sew on fish and seaweed to fronts. Add eyes to fish using black yarn.

Little Rosebud Wrap Set

Every baby girl needs an outfit for a special occasion, and this pretty wrap top, bonnet, and shoes are just perfect for an outing. Delicate embroidered roses embellish the pieces, and they are tied with matching satin ribbon. I have chosen cream edged with a pretty burgundy color, but you can chose whatever color combination you like from the vast array of shades available in this yarn.

Materials

- Sirdar Snuggly DK (light worsted weight)
  - 4 x 50g balls in shade 303 Cream (yarn A)
  - 1 x 50g ball in shade 484 Cherry Pie (yarn B)
- Small amount of green DK yarn for embroidery
- Knitting needles sizes 3.25mm (US 3, UK 10) and 3.75mm (US 4, UK 9)
- Large-eyed sewing needle
- Matching narrow double-sided ribbon, approx. 3 yds. (3m)

Gauge: 24 sts x 42 rows measures 4 in. (10cm) using 3.75mm (US 4, UK 9) needles

Measurements: To fit ages 0–3 months. Chest is 16 in. (41cm); length is 9 in. (23cm); sleeve seam is 2 in. (5cm); width around face of bonnet is 12½ in. (32cm).

Abbreviations: See page 27

Special Abbreviation: k2togtbl = knit 2 stitches together through the back loops

Back

Using 3.75mm (US 4, UK 9) needles and yarn B, cast on 57 sts.

Knit 7 rows in garter stitch. Change to yarn A.

Work in garter stitch for 5 in. (12cm) from beg, ending on WS row.

SHAPE RAGLAN ARMHOLES

Bind off 3 sts at beg of next 2 rows.

Next Row: K2, k2tog tbl, k to last 4 sts, k2tog, k2.

Next Row: Knit.

Rep last 2 rows until you have 19 sts.

Leave on holder for Back Neck.

SLEEVES (MAKE 2 ALIKE)

Using 3.75mm (US 4, UK 9) needles and B, cast on 47 sts.

Knit 7 rows in garter stitch. Change to A.

Change to stockinette stitch and continue until work measures 2 in. (5cm).

SHAPE RAGLAN ARMHOLES

Bind off 3 sts at beg of next 2 rows.

Next Row: K2, k2togtbl, k to last 4 sts, k2tog, k2.

Next Row: K2, k2tog, k to last 4 sts, k2togtbl, k2.

Rep last 2 rows once more.

Next Row: K2, k2togtbl, k to last 4 sts, k2tog, k2.

Next Row: Knit.

Rep last 2 rows to 9 sts, break yarn, and leave sts on holder.

Left Front

Using 3.75mm (US 4, UK 9) needles and B, cast on 28 sts.

Work 7 rows in garter stitch.

Change to A and work to match back to armhole shaping, ending on a WS row.

SHAPE RAGLAN ARMHOLES

Bind off 3 sts at beg of next row.

Next Row: Knit.

Next Row: K2, k2tog, k to end.

Next Row: Knit.

Continue as set on last 2 rows until you have 15 sts.

Work 1 row, ending on a WS row.

SHAPE NECK

Next Row: K2, k2tog, work to last 6 sts. Turn (slip 6 sts onto holder)

Next Row: Knit.

Dec 1 st at neck edge on next 2 alt rows, and at the same time dec at Armhole Edge as before until 2 sts rem; work 2tog and fasten off.

Right Front

Using 3.75mm (US 4, UK 9) needles and B, cast on 36 sts.

Work 7 rows in garter stitch.

Change to A and work to match back to armhole shaping, ending on a RS row.

SHAPE RAGLAN ARMHOLE

Bind off 3 sts at beg of next row.

Dec 1 st at raglan edge on next and every foll alt row until you have 23 sts.

SHAPE NECK

Bind off 6 sts, work to last 4 sts, k2tog tbl, k2.

Dec 1 st at neck edge on next 2 alt rows, and at the same time dec as before at armhole edge until 2 sts rem; work 2tog and fasten off.

Sew raglan seams.

Front Edgings

RIGHT FRONT

Using 3.25mm (US 3, UK 10) needles and B, with right side facing, begin at lower edge and pick up and k44 sts evenly along edge. Work 6 rows in garter stitch and bind off.

LEFT FRONT

Work to match right front, but begin at top edge when picking up sts.

NECK EDGE

Using 3.25mm (US 3, UK 10) needles and B, pick up and k28 sts from right Front Neck, 9 sts from Sleeve, 19 sts from Back, 9 sts from Sleeve, and 22 sts from Left Front.

Next Row: Knit.
Next Row: K10, k2tog, k1, k2togtbl, work to last 15 sts, k2togtbl, k1, k2tog, k10.
Next Row: Knit.
Next Row: K10, k2tog, k1, k2togtbl, work to 15 sts, k2togtbl, k1, k2tog, k1.
Next Row: Knit.
Next Row: K10, k2tog, k1, k2togtbl, work to 15 sts, k2togtbl, k1, k2tog, k1.
Next Row: Knit.
Bind off.

RIBBON LOOPS (MAKE 2 ALIKE)

Using 3.75mm (US 4, UK 9) needles and B, cast on 20 sts. Bind off.

Finishing

Work in ends neatly. Join side and sleeve seams, matching colored stripes.

Sew buttons loops onto right front edge using photo for placement.

Cut two equal lengths of ribbon. Fold in half and stitch onto front to correspond with ribbon loops.

Thread one end of ribbon through loops and tie into a bow. Using B, embroider a rose using bullion stitch onto one front. Take some green yarn and embroider leaves.

Bonnet

Using 3.25mm (US 3, UK 10) needles and yarn B, cast on 72 sts.
Work in garter stitch for 7 rows.
Change to 3.75mm (US 4, UK 9)
    needles and A. Work in garter stitch until piece measures 5½ in. (14cm).

SHAPE CROWN

Change to B.
Row 1: * K10, skp, rep from * across row.
Row 2 and alt (even-numbered) foll rows: Knit.
Row 3: * K9, skp, rep from * across row.
Row 5: * K8, skp, rep from * across row.
Row 7: * K7, skp, rep from * across row.
Row 9: * K6, skp, rep from * across row.
Row 11: * K5, skp, rep from * across row.
Row 13: * K4, skp, rep from * across row.
Row 15: * K3, skp, rep from * across row.
Row 17: * K2, skp, rep from * across row.

Row 19: * K1, skp, rep from *
across row.

Row 20: K2tog across row. Break yarn
and run through sts on needle, draw
up, and fasten off.

TIES (MAKE 2 ALIKE)

Using 3.25mm (US 3, UK 10) needles
and yarn B, cast on 5 sts.

Work in garter stitch until piece
measures 8 in. (20cm). Bind off.

Sew back seam on garter stitch,
shaping on back of bonnet. Sew a
tie to each side of the bonnet.

Using yarn B, embroider a rose with
a bullion stitch and add leaves in
green yarn.

Crossover Shoes

Using 3.25mm (US 4, UK 10) needles
and B, cast on 9 sts.

Next Row: Knit.

BEGIN TO SHAPE SOLE AS FOLLOWS

Row 1: Kfb at each end of the row
(11 sts).

Row 2: Knit.

Row 3: Kfb at each end of row (13 sts).

Rows 4–10: Knit.

Row 11: Inc 1 st at each end of the row
(15 sts).

Rows 12–22: Knit.

Row 23: Inc 1 st at each end of row
(17 sts).

Rows 24–36: Knit.

NOW SHAPE TOE AS FOLLOWS

Row 37: K2tog at each end of row.

Row 38: Knit.

Now work k2tog at each end of the
next 3 rows (9 sts).

Bind off. This is the toe end of
the sole.

UPPER PART OF SHOE (CAST ON EDGE IS BOTTOM EDGE OF PIECE)

Using 3.25mm (US 3, UK 10) needles
  and A, cast on 57 sts loosely.
Work 16 rows in garter stitch.

SHAPE OVERLAPS

Row 1: Work k2tog at each end of row.
Row 2: Rep row 1.
Row 3: Knit.
Row 4: Work k2tog at each end of row.
Join in B and k1 row. Bind off.

BUTTON LOOPS (MAKE 2)

Using 3.25mm (US 3, UK 10) needles
  and B, cast on 16 sts. Bind off.

Finishing

Take upper part of shoe and pin
cast-on edge in place around outer
edge of sole. Overlap the two ends at
the front of the shoe, left over right on
one shoe, and right over left on the
other. Sew in place carefully, easing a
little if needed at the rounded toe end
of the shoe. (It will take a little time and
patience to get the fit neat.) Embroider
a rose onto the side of each shoe in
the same way as before.

Sew a button loop onto side of
shoe. Cut a length of ribbon and fold
in half. Sew onto side of shoe, thread
one end through loop, and tie in a
bow. Rep with other shoe.

Index

Note: Page numbers in *italics* indicate projects.

Suppliers

Yarn Brands

The following brands were used to make the projects for this book.

CARON

www.yarnspirations.com

KING COLE

www.kingcole.com

RICO

www.rico-design.de

SIRDAR

www.sirdar.co.uk

North America

All suppliers listed ship internationally unless otherwise stated.

BLACK SHEEP WOOLS

www.blacksheepwools.com
A family-owned business, Black Sheep Wools sells yarn, patterns, books, and accessories.

JIMMY BEANS WOOL

www.jimmybeanswool.com
This retailer sells yarn, needles, patterns, kits, and notions.

KNIT-N-CROCHET

www.knit-n-crochet.com
This retailer sells a wide variety of specialty yarns, kits, and knitting and crochet supplies.

KNIT PICKS

www.knitpicks.com
Knit Picks sells yarns and fibers, kits, knitting and crochet supplies, patterns, and books. They also offer several different types of knitting and crochet project subscription boxes.

KNITTING-WAREHOUSE

www.knitting-warehouse.com
This discount knitting retailer is based in Michigan, USA. It's an excellent source for purchasing yarns, knitting and crochet supplies, kits, and books. Ships to the USA and Canada.

LOVE KNITTING

www.loveknitting.com
Love Knitting offers a multitude of brands, patterns, tools, kits, and how-to tutorials for knitting techniques.

WEBS

www.yarn.com
This family-owned business sells an assortment of yarn brands, patterns, kits, and knitting essentials.

YARNSPIRATIONS

www.yarnspirations.com
Yarnspirations sells yarn (including Caron brand), knit and crochet patterns, and accessories. They also offer educational videos and a blog that can be a great source for inspiration.

United Kingdom/Europe

DERAMORES

www.deramores.com
This UK-based online store sells yarn, patterns, and needle working supplies. Deramores also sells kits for making clothes, blankets, home décor items, and stuffed animals.

ENGLISH YARNS

www.englishyarns.co.uk
English Yarns sells a range of yarns, patterns, and supplies. Also, if you're on the lookout for discontinued Rowan, Sublime, Regia, Patons, and Sirdar yarns and patterns, this online retailer is the place to go.

GREAT BRITISH YARNS

www.greatbritishyarns.co.uk
This small business takes pride in providing a carefully curated selection of yarns that includes materials from various independent yarn dyers. They also sell knitting patterns and tools.

HOBBII

www.hobbii.co.uk
This Denmark-based company sells yarns, accessories, and supplies. They also offer free patterns created by their own Scandinavian designers.

STYLECRAFT

www.stylecraft-yarns.co.uk
Stylecraft is a family-run business that offers on-trend yarns and patterns, in addition to their collection of timeless materials and designs that knitters have enjoyed time and again.

VIRIDIAN

www.viridianyarn.com
Viridian is an online retailer that sells yarns, craft products, and accessories. They are also the exclusive seller of Opal, a brand famous for its yarn that is dyed in such a way to help knitters create striped socks with zero effort on their part.

WOOL WAREHOUSE

www.woolwarehouse.co.uk
Wool Warehouse is an independent retailer that sells everything a knitter needs, from yarn to accessories. They mostly do their business online, but still have a physical location in Leamington Spa.

Acknowledgments

Firstly, I would like to thank Fox Chapel Publishing for the giving me the opportunity to write this lovely book. Many thanks also go to Tiffany Hill, Katie Ocasio, and Wendy Reynolds for their help, inspiration, and hard work in putting together all the aspects for this book, including the beautiful photographs that display the projects.

Many thanks go to Rico, King Cole, Caron, and Sirdar for kindly providing their amazing yarns used to knit the projects.

And finally thanks go to my friends and family for their encouragement and help given to me when designing and making all the projects featured.

Photo Credits

Images from *Shutterstock.com*: IhorZigor (yarn ball clipart 2, all project opener pages); mama_mia (2–3); PinkPueblo (baby carriage illustrations 4, 24, 144); keri_aa (hanging socks illustration 5, 7, 8, 138, 140, 142, 144); Anfisa Che (yarn basket and knitting needles 6–7); LightField Studios (8 bottom); V.S.Anandhakrishna (9); Natalia Pyzhova (10); Tarzhanova (metal needles 11); Anastasia E Kozlova (plastic needles 11); Melica (12, 28–29, 143); Crepesoles (14 bottom); munalin (19); BW Folsom (23 bottom); bright (26); and Kostikova Natalia (139).

Text, step-by-step photography on pages 13–24, and photo on page 21 reproduced from *Cutest Ever Baby Knits* by Val Pierce and published by IMM Lifestyle Books.

Project photography on jacket, pages 4–5, and pages 31–137 by Mike Mihalo.

About the Author

Val Pierce's passion for knitting began when her father taught her to knit at the age of five. Later in life, she began home knitting for yarn manufacturers, and since then she has made a huge range of items, from evening dresses to teddy bears. She later began designing items of her own, and before long, her dreams were appearing in knitting and crochet magazines. She also teaches knitting and crochet to both adults and children.